The Irish King of Winter Hill

The True Story of
James J. "Buddy" McLean

The Irish King of Winter Hill

The True Story of
James J. "Buddy" McLean

Written by

Michael McLean

Strategic Book Publishing and Rights Co.

Strategic Book Publishing and Rights Co.
12620 FM 1960, Suite A4-507
Houston TX 77065
www.sbpra.com

ISBN: 978-1-62516-669-2

DEDICATION

Dedicated to my dad and the family and friends remaining who fondly remember "The Irish King"

CONTENTS

PREFACE

McLean-McLaughlin Irish Gang War.
The Boston Irish Gang War started in 1961 and lasted until 1966. It was fought between the McLaughlins of Charlestown, led by Bernie McLaughlin, and the Winter Hill Gang of Somerville, led by the KING, James "Buddy" McLean. The two gangs had co-existed, with strained respect, in relative peace until an incident Labor Day weekend 1961 in Salisbury Beach.

Buddy was ultimately dragged into a situation that had nothing to do with him. But being the honorable stand-up guy that he was, Buddy would never turn his back on his friends. Thus was the beginning of the bloodiest gang war in American history.

The Irish who lived in Somerville and Charlestown were at war with one another. The war took well over one hundred lives (seventy deaths were recorded, with others reported missing). This happened in just under a five-year period. This war will be remembered as the bloodiest organized Irish crime gang war in American history to date. Not since the Chicago gang wars of the roaring twenties had so many died. This all started over the defense of a woman. The incident had taken place in a small summer beach resort town of Salisbury Beach, Massachusetts, on Labor Day weekend 1961. In 1965, Buddy McLean was shot and killed by one of the last survivors of the McLaughlin Gang, Steve Hughes. A year later to the date, after more than one hundred dead or missing, the last two associates of the McLaughlin Gang, brothers Connie and Steve Hughes, were found dead.

When the KING died, so did loyalty, dignity, and respect. The Winter Hill Gang also died that day, never to be the same again. Buddy McLean was Winter Hill.

The Winter Hill Gang was then taken over by men who could not fill the KING's shoes, men who knew nothing about respect or, more importantly, loyalty, the two most important things the KING built his reputation on.

INTRODUCTION

This is the true story of the rise and fall of the first "Irish King" of Winter Hill, James J. "Buddy" McLean, who led the original and infamous Winter Hill Gang.

In 1961, in the small resort town of Salisbury, Massachusetts, an Irish gangster by the name of George McLaughlin (Georgie) made a drunken, obnoxious pass at the wife of a small-time Somerville bookie named Frank. A drunken Georgie continually terrorized the guests. As a result, George McLaughlin was beaten with whiskey bottles and sustained massive head injuries. Frank and a friend of his by the name of Ed were responsible for the beating. The McLaughlin brothers from Charlestown, Massachusetts, consisted of Bernie, Edward "Punchy," and Georgie, the smallest and youngest of the brothers. When the two elder McLaughlins learned what happened, they immediately drove to Salisbury Beach and wanted to shed blood themselves. Ed and Frank would both have been dead, except for one thing—a union teamster truck driver from Local #25 in Charlestown, a man by the name of James J. "Buddy" McLean, the Irish King from Winter Hill in Somerville, Massachusetts. Buddy had a wife and four small children by the time of the Salisbury Beach incident. Buddy was ultimately dragged into a situation that had nothing to do with him. Honorable and loyal, the King would never turn his back on his friends, and he didn't. Thus was the beginning of one of the bloodiest gang wars in American history to date.

Okay, so now you know how it ended, let me tell you how it all began.

The events you are about to read are based on a true story, never told till now.

Some names and dates have been changed or eliminated to protect the guilty.

ONE

Buddy was born January 26, 1930, in Boston, Massachusetts, to longshoreman William McLean, of Irish descent, and Dorothy Guida, of German descent. A few months after James was born Dorothy became ill; she asked her neighbor Doris Raposa to watch her son while she was in the hospital, as Doris and Dorothy had become friends during the pregnancy. Doris of course said yes, however, being very young, and not knowing how to take care of a small child, Doris went to her Portuguese grandmother, Mary Raposa, who lived in Somerville, for assistance. Mary, who fell in love with James at first sight, was more than willing to help. Not knowing the situation, Mary welcomed Buddy into her home with open arms.

Mary loved Buddy and treated him like her own son, and Buddy idolized Mary. Life in Somerville was very different in the thirties and forties—the residents were mostly Irish blue-collar workers. Most of the families had three and four children, and some had many more, and almost all were Catholic. The fathers were the breadwinners, and the mothers all stayed home to care for the kids and to keep the house in order. Children of two working parents were left to the streets after school; between the hours of three and five, the punks ran the streets.

Buddy's father, Bill, did come around once and awhile and give Mary money to help her with Buddy's expenses. Knowing Buddy's mother would never return and believing he could not be a constant father figure for Buddy, Bill McLean made himself scarce. Being a longshoreman he would, when the time came, give his son his union card, the only legacy he could leave. Bill was well liked on the docks. He was good to everyone, and everyone respected him. He knew his son would be well received, and a union card was worth more than saving gold for him.

Buddy grew up on the streets of Somerville. He learned the streets the hard way. By the age of nine Buddy could hold his own in a street fight, and finding the YMCA was the best thing that happened to him. He worked out every day after school, watching the big guys and following along with them. He got into his own routine of hitting the bag and doing hundreds of pushups; his muscles and stamina always kept him going in a fight. By the time he was twelve he had a reputation for being an extremely tough street fighter who never lost a fight. It seemed he could go on forever.

He always remembered what his father told him: "You want to know if it's the truth, look in their eyes. The eyes will always tell you if they are telling you the truth!" Buddy always had that innocent look about him that he always used to his advantage. When he asked you a question, he demanded the truth with just his eyes. Unfortunately, he had to beat a few asses to get the truth, but in the end he always got it and earned the respect of the beaten.

He would tell them, "If you had told the truth in the beginning, it would have saved me all this beating shit . . . next time just tell me the truth, but I'm only going to ask you once!"

As the years went on he had earned the respect of many a man without one punch being thrown, but then there were those who thought they could test him. Buddy was never a violent man. He didn't want these fights, but they just seemed to come to him. He had to fight his way through many of the early years because of his size (he was small for his age), so some thought he could be bullied. Boy, were they wrong.

TWO

At thirteen Buddy was driving a truck. Most able-bodied men were away fighting the war at that time, so there were many jobs available on the docks to teenagers. Pat Kelligan, Laura Raposa's husband (Laura is sister to Doris and granddaughter to Mary), let Buddy go to work with him as soon as he could reach the gas peddles. Pat taught him how to drive trailers in open parking lots on Saturdays and Sundays. JM Fields parking lot was Buddy's favorite. He could actually drive all around the building, teaching himself how to control the rear body of the truck. Buddy caught on quickly and could drive just as well as, or better than, any of the seasoned truckers.

At fourteen, while hanging out on his corner with his lifelong friend Martin "Puska" Murphy (who later became Massachusetts state police captain) and Puska's brother Vinnie, he met Jean Kelly, the woman he knew he would marry. She was beautiful; Buddy took one look at her and was hooked. She was his dream—blonde hair, blue eyes, and she was certainly built. She made him feel like being a better man, as if he could do anything. Her smile would soften any man's heart, especially Buddy's. His knees would go weak, and he would immediately start daydreaming. He could never put the feeling into words, but he liked how she made him feel. Every time he would see her and that smile of hers that warm feeling would overwhelm him. Jean made life worth living. He would rush his days just so he could see that smile and know he was safe with his Jean.

Getting his driving permit at the age of fifteen, Buddy drove a pickup truck for the electric company. He saved up all his money and bought himself a motorcycle and a '42 Plymouth so that he and Jean could go for long rides together. However, the Plymouth didn't last long after getting cut off. Buddy rolled it over coming back from a friend's home in Bangor, Maine. The car was totaled, but Buddy didn't really care—cars were not really his thing.

Jean was of Irish decent and had two brothers and four sisters. She lived in the Winter Hill area where Buddy also lived. Buddy and Jean attended Foster Elementary School, but Buddy didn't remember her from there. She had flourished between then and when he saw her passing by him on the corner. They went on to Northeastern Junior High together, and that's where Buddy really fell hard. Jean had really matured in those few years. She had turned into an absolute beauty to Buddy. All Buddy had to do to make her his was to convince her two brothers that he was in love with their sister, that she was his whole world, and that he would make sure she never wanted for anything. In those days it was respectful to get permission from the family, and Buddy knew that they probably had heard of him but really didn't know him, or so he thought. Jean's two brothers had heard that Buddy was a stand-up man, that he was honorable and a force to be reckoned with. With his reputation of being a great street fighter, they knew Jean would be safe. They also knew he was a man who believed what was right was right, and what was wrong should be made right. He was well known and respected on the streets. His reputation had many facets: he would never turn his back on anyone who needed help, and if he was there, and he could help, he helped, whether it be a stranger or a friend. He always lent a hand or gave what was needed at the time.

Of course both brothers and all four sisters gave their blessing, as did her mother. Once Buddy had the approval of the whole family, Jean was forever known as Buddy's girl. Buddy of course escorted Jean to their junior prom. They then went on to attend Somerville High together. In his sophomore year Buddy quit school to try to become a teamster in local #25. But he always had time for his Jean, and he did escort Jean to what should have been their senior prom. Buddy and Jean used to attend movies together up at the Capital Movie Theater on Broadway in Winter Hill. They were almost regulars. He would take her any place she wanted to go, and Buddy would make sure she got anything else she wanted. Jean and Buddy were married as soon as Jean graduated, and they began working on their family.

THREE

At nineteen, Buddy started to work for Fay Transportation, loading and unloading trucks. Every night after work he used to run laps around Tuft's Park. He loved the dirt trail they had there. When I was old enough I would get to run with him, usually on a day I didn't have school. We would run regardless of the sun beating down on us. He taught me how to run, and he taught me stamina and how to keep going even when you think you can't run anymore. We would do a few laps together, and every time I got better and better at being able to do more and more laps before I would have to stop. I would sit there and watch as he kept running around and around, sweat pouring off him, and I would think that someday I'd be able to run like that. Thanks to my dad I do run like that, every day, and he is running right beside me as we did back then. He is with me every step, which keeps me going. And when I think I can't run anymore, I hear his voice in my head, saying, "Keep going, Michael, just one more lap!"

During those summers after his run he would drop me off at home and go to Foss Park and swim several laps in their regulation size pool, which I couldn't swim in yet. He also did hundreds of pushups and sit-ups daily, some at home before he left the house to go to the Y to hit the bag. To get us into working out he put a chin-up bar up so my brother and I could compete doing chin-ups every morning before school.

"Just to loosen up," Dad would say, and "Keeps you limber." I remember him calling us and saying, "It's time guys. Let's see who's gonna win today." He would then smile and wink at me. It was fun. Jimmy and I would both do our best, but Jimmy always won. After all, he was older. But I was getting stronger, and my dad would always say to me, "Someday, Michael, you will beat him," and he would then lovingly pat me on the head. Then, off to school we went, both of us happy with ourselves for pleasing Dad. It wasn't till years later that I did beat my brother. My dad was right; he would have been proud to see me finally beat Jimmy. He would then go off to the Y and do multiple rounds on the bag just to keep him on his toes. He did this because of his amateur boxing experience, which was his passion. Keeping limber and his unending stamina he got from running were his secrets to winning in a street fight.

FOUR

He loved sports, any sport—didn't matter to him. It was a great way to expel his excess energy and build muscle. He was tough, and everybody knew it—it took many a street fight to prove it—and Buddy never lost a fight. He met some very influential people during these fights, for example after a game that was being played by the Somerville Rams, who were the number one amateur football team in the Greater Boston Area, being coached by John Hurley, and Buddy's 10 Hill Squad. These two teams had become rivals, and as many times as they would play, unfortunately Buddy's 10 Hill team would never win a game.

After a really tough game John and Buddy went into the locker room to get changed. They sat facing each other on the old wooden benches. Buddy's 10 Hill Squad had just lost yet another game. The game had been close right up until the last touchdown. Both sides played as if it were for all the marbles. Even so, the 10 Hill Squad could not beat the Rams. When Buddy bent down to take his shoes off, both he and John butted heads, each thinking the other had done it on purpose. Of course, they exchanged a few words, and both boys had to protect their honor, so into battle they went. With all the pushing, shoving, and name calling going on the two boys had moved outside on the grass, where they had more room. There the real fight began.

Finally, after what seemed to be forever, which was only about ten minutes, the equipment manager at the park, Harry, who had been watching the fight and who saw that the fight was going nowhere, decided to stop it. He started yelling at the boys.

"Okay, guys, break it up." He came between the two boys. "This fight is over. C'mon, you guys, shake hands now, and let's just call it a draw."

There were a lot of bumps, bruises, and blood—the two boys did put on a good showing. Harry knew that the fight was in Buddy's favor at this point, so why not stop it now and tell the boys it was a draw so they wouldn't continue it another day? To Harry's surprise, after stopping the fight when he did, the two boys had become friends.

After the fight John and Buddy had become friends. They earned each other's respect and friendship, which lasted till the death of the King, and to the day of John's death. Buddy admired John; he stood up well under all the punches and never complained. It had been a fair fight. John remembers waking up the next day thinking that, had the fight gone on any longer, he couldn't have held up any more under all of Buddy's body blows. He was barely able to hold his arms up when Harry had stopped it. John knew that Buddy was winning, but this way it would be a tie, and no one would know the truth (but John!).

John already had a reputation on the docks. He recalled an incident that would change his life forever.

"We were just twelve years old. Tommy Ballou, Tommy Birmingham and I were just hanging down on Commonwealth Pier, but we were also working at the docks due to the shortage of man power in the middle of WWII. We heard a ruckus coming from the nearby longshoreman's union owned building. Being young, we went in to investigate. We looked up the stairway and saw two guys wearing ski masks trying to rob the timekeeper of the payroll. As we moved in closer the timekeeper saw us and charged at the two men. The gun went flying out of the robber's hand and came bouncing down the stairs. Tommy Ballou picked it up and shot one of the robbers. With this the two men took off running. We were heroes around the docks from that day on. The union put the word out that we saved the timekeeper's life, and if anyone fucked with any of us, they would never work again. After the shooting, the union officials bought us an ice cream, and that was that. They never reported it to the police. One minute three twelve-year-old kids got to shoot a guy, and the next we were walking around eating ice cream, like nothing had happened. Buddy in later years also became a friend of Tommy Ballou."

One night the owner of a bar in South Boston called Buddy and told him that Big Jim, John's father, had been drinking too much, and he was worried about his safety. Without hesitation, Buddy and Tommy Ballou went to South Boston to pick him up and take him home.

They put Big Jim in the back seat and proceeded to take him home. Buddy and Tommy held Big Jim between them as they knocked on the front door. When John's mother opened the door, there stood the two men holding up the drunken Jim. Seeing Jim's condition, Mary allowed the men to enter. Tommy threw Big Jim over his shoulder while Buddy carried a case of beer and two bottles of whiskey.

"Sorry," Buddy said. "The alcohol was the only way we could get Jim to come home." Mary directed Tommy to their bedroom. After he placed Jim on the bed Mary motioned for him and Buddy to go into the kitchen.

She understood about the booze and thanked Buddy for his effort. Tommy and Buddy were about to leave when Mary insisted that she have a word with Buddy.

So Tommy said, "I'll wait for you in the car, Buddy," and left.

Mary sat at the kitchen table and motioned for Buddy to do the same. She enjoyed a cup of tea and had placed some homemade cookies on a saucer in front of Buddy. She began by telling Buddy how she knew that John was involved with all this gang war stuff even though he assured his mother he had nothing to do with it. Mary also told Buddy that she knew her husband, Jim, was also involved with the gang war, but he wouldn't admit it either.

That's when she hit Buddy with, "I know everything that's going on in Charlestown with my Irish connections! I have something I need to tell you. I am only telling you this to protect my Jim and John." John had just come walking into the house at this point. Mary told him he needed to go back to the Capitol Café with Tommy, that she was having a word with Buddy, and that Buddy would be up when she was done with him.

When John came out and told Tommy what his mother said, Tommy told John, "You go ahead, John. I'm gonna wait for Buddy, and we'll be up when he's done." John went to the Capitol, and Tommy continued to wait in the car, wondering what she could be telling him that only he could hear. Mary was not stupid; she knew the information that she was passing on to Buddy could get her killed, but she didn't care at this point—she had to protect her family. Her telling Buddy what she knew would give him the upper hand in all this, and no one would ever suspect her.

After what seemed to be hours Tommy and Buddy came walking into the Capitol Café. They had just passed Leo, who was going to drop off his brother, Joe McDonald, wherever he was hiding out at the time. Buddy told Joe he would be by later, and that he had some interesting information he should know. So Buddy and Tommy walked in and told John to follow them into the back room.

When they got there, Buddy told John, "All the years I've known your mother, I never thought she had that kind of information." She was a sly woman, ears always listening, eyes always watching, and all her friends were the same, nice, old Irish ladies, always smiling. She told Buddy he could tell John certain things, and that was all. Buddy chose carefully what he told John, or Tommy, for that matter. He thought to keep some stuff to himself, which was in his best interest.

Mary's sister had been dating Mike Kelly, who was partners with Jimmy Preston, the biggest Irish gangster in Massachusetts during the twenties, thirties, forties, and early fifties. There were also two more powerful Irish families in Charlestown she thought he should know about, the O'Neil and McAvoy clans. She knew when Preston retired he sold all the families businesses and ventures to the McLaughlins. They took over all of the booking, loansharking, check cashing, and any other dirty deeds that needed doing. There were only three check cashing places in Charlestown back then. Two were in tobacco stores, and the other was McAvoy's bar. No other bars or stores were allowed to cash checks, and the three that did had to pay Preston his due. She knew of the many connections that most people were unaware of. Between Mary and her sister they put together a pretty good amount of information for Buddy. John seemed happy with what Buddy had told him and really didn't question Buddy for more information than Buddy was willing to give. After leaving the club and heading to see Joe, with all this new found information, Buddy was amazed at what Mary had told him, the things he couldn't tell John or Tommy or, for that matter, anyone.

Later that night Buddy sat with Joe in his kitchen discussing some of the information he had just received from Mary. He was telling Joe things Joe thought he already knew. Mary knew much more about the McLaughlins and the other clans in Charlestown than Joe.

FIVE

At twenty Buddy started his own "trucking company" with his friend Bob Mahoney. The company was named Travelers Transportation and is still going strong to this day, run by Bob Mahoney's son, now under the names Travelers Transportation and Ocean Transfer.

They had only one truck when they started out, running their operation out of the Trucking Combine in South Boston. He would drive that one truck everywhere, taking turns with his partner Bob. The men would drive as far as the Dakotas or even to California if they had the chance. Buddy was always hustling and rushing every job, just to get home to Jean and that smile that always kept him motivated. I remember when he would do what he called "runs" on a Saturday, and I would get to go with him. It meant driving to Gloucester to pick up live lobsters, then delivering them to the fish pier, and if we were lucky fishing off the pier afterward. The drive to Gloucester was always filled with chatter between us. We talked about everything: sports, school, boxing—just man talk. I remember when he wanted to make me laugh he would squeeze my knee, right where I was ticklish, and I would giggle, and we would both laugh. The drive was always the same—chatter and giggles. I loved it when I got to go with him. We would pick up the boxes of lobsters and then the same chatter and giggles all the way to the fish pier. When we got home, he would give me some of the leftover lobsters and tell me to take them around the neighborhood.

Charlie across the street yelled after me one time, "Hey, Michael, I can't take these."

And I yelled back, "My dad said I couldn't take them back, so you're gonna have to keep them." Going anywhere with my Dad back then was always fascinating to me, to see how people treated him. He was somebody special to them, and it showed. I always thought everyone got to eat free at the places we would go. We did. I don't ever remember my Dad paying for anything, but he always left a good tip.

Weekends went too fast for us kids. Dad worked so hard during the week that we only got to see him on the weekends. Once a month or so we would get to go to the drive-in, on a Saturday that he didn't have to work, with Little Nicky, a good friend of my dad's. Little Nicky was a running friend of my dad. They ran almost every day together, but that's another story. We had a ball there. We got to go play on the amusements before the movie started, and then Dad and Little Nicky would go to the concession stand and bring us back all kinds of goodies.

If he had to work on a Saturday at the fish pier, unloading the gypsy truckers from Canada, and up and down the coastline, they always requested my dad and his crew because they knew that they would get a better price. Buddy wouldn't let the buyers take advantage of them. If I was lucky I'd get to go with him. After he was done we would get to go fishing behind the old no-name restaurant. He would finish his work and then take a couple of fishing poles from his friend Satch's trunk, and the two of us would fish. We rarely caught anything, but just sitting there on the pier in the sun with my Dad was the best way to spend a Saturday afternoon. He would tell me about the gypsy truckers and their fishing stories, and how they had to drive down here to get the best price, and that they were used to fishing in below zero temperatures, not like the fishermen in Gloucester, and they usually had quite a good catch.

Monday was always my least favorite day. I had to go to school, and my dad had to go to work twelve hours a day just to get his company going. And if the company got a job, it usually meant Dad wouldn't be home for a few days, which made the week even longer.

SIX

Buddy and Bob worked tirelessly for months till Buddy got a drop off in New York, which he promptly took. Opening up the east coast was what he had hoped for. He knew it would be hard at first working with the teamsters, but that didn't stop him. He knew he had to open up New York—it was the place to be, and he knew the future of his trucking business depended on this run.

The drive to New York was uneventful for Buddy and very boring; however, while Buddy was making the delivery to the New York waterfront, he met Harold Farmer, a well liked New York enforcer and very dangerous man. Harold was cruising the docks that day, looking to harass some of the new drivers. Harold spotted Buddy unloading his truck and started a conversation with him. They talked for several minutes while his muscle men watched, waiting for their signal. With all the smiles and handshakes it looked as if Harold took a liking to the blond haired, blue eyed, baby faced Buddy after this one meeting. This meeting was pivotal to the teamsters in Boston being able to go to New York with their deliveries and pick up loads for return to Boston. Harold told Buddy he was welcome to come back and deliver if he needed to, that he would keep his goons at bay. Finding Buddy to be a straightforward and hardworking man, Harold became instant friends with Buddy with just a hand shake and that look in Buddy's eyes, which was worth more than Buddy's word.

Harold took such a liking to Buddy he waved his men off and told them, "Let this kid deliver. We can catch him again later." Buddy made his delivery and picked up the returning load. He was ecstatic that he had no problems this run. No one bothered him, and meeting Harold certainly didn't hurt. He headed home, hoping for another chance at New York. With this run having gone so well he knew it wouldn't be long.

And it wasn't. When other companies that were trying to get their goods to New York heard of his delivery without incident, they were eager to hire Travelers Transportation.

After meeting Buddy, Harold had spread the word with his associates, telling them he was a good kid, that maybe he could be recruited later. Unbeknownst to the McLaughlins, their good buddy Harold Farmer would secretly be backing Buddy during the war, as would some of the McLaughlins New York Irish mobsters.

Buddy finally had the chance for Travelers Transportation to go to Albany, New York, for a drop off and pick up of goods to be delivered to Maryland. Buddy knew this could be a tough delivery, as Albany was one hundred percent run by the Italian mob. Buddy had heard stories about Albany, how the mob ran the docks there, and no driver got in or out without paying their fee, which would take most of the profits from the drivers who were just trying to make a buck to feed their families.

If you didn't pay, the mob would either break legs and/or destroy their trucks. Being aware of all this didn't stop Buddy; he was determined to open up Albany for the teamsters and every driver that had to stop there. The job was to stop in Albany to make a seafood delivery and then pick up other perishables, continue on to Maryland and then back to Boston. It was a long trip. Two men would have to take the ride, and it was Buddy's turn. His partner, Bob, had just returned from the west coast, a longer trip than this. So Buddy decided to take a helper with him, Ryan. Ryan, who was more muscle than brains but was a great worker and good company, would always be Buddy's first choice. Ryan always did what he was told, no questions asked. Taking Ryan would give Bob a chance to rest, because if things went as well as Buddy hoped it could mean a lot of work for Travelers Transportation.

Buddy liked Ryan's company. He knew everything you wanted to know about boxing. It amazed Buddy. Buddy always enjoyed listening to Ryan describe each fight round by round, which always made the trips go faster.

He never told Jean how dangerous these trips were. He didn't want her to worry. Besides, she made all the hard work worth it, knowing he could walk in the house and Jean would be there with that smile on her face and dinner on the table. The kids being all excited to have him home was the best feeling in the world.

Buddy believed in spending as much time with his kids as possible. Every Saturday morning he would take us for a few games at the bowling alley behind Leone's on the Hill. They always saved a lane for Buddy just in case he came in.

If anyone wanted to talk to him while we were there, he would always tell them, "See me later. Can't you see I'm with my kids right now?" My dad made just going up to the corner drug store for an ice cream worth it. He would joke with us, and he was always finding something funny for us to laugh about. We enjoyed it so and loved just being with him.

During the drive Buddy and Ryan talked endlessly about different boxing matches that had taken place. Another reason for bringing Ryan was that he was strong and could hold his own if they encountered any problems along the way. Buddy had seen Ryan when angered, which was why he chose Ryan to go with him. Besides, he liked his company.

When they arrived at the Albany Trucking Combine, Buddy was approached by a man belonging to Albany's local Italian muscle. He didn't take the time to introduce himself, the man who was of Italian descent with the obvious look of a typical mob boss mouthpiece, more muscle than brains. He folded his massive arms in front of him and stood there like a brick shithouse dressed in a too-small silk suit. He explained Albany's "rules and regulations" to Buddy. He told them it was okay to drop stuff off, but if they were going to take anything out with them, they would have to pay a special fee, and that he was going to be their broker. Nothing went in or out without paying the fee to the local mob. In other words, they were doing in New York what the McLaughlins failed to do in Boston—shaking down the truck drivers.

The Irish worked New York's West Side as well as the entire waterfront. A large percentage of the waterfront profits came from the daily ten-to-twenty percent work fees that the union hiring foreman charged its members for an honest day's work. To help pay these fees the workers could turn to the loan sharks who were standing on the ready, but they also required a fee of their own. In Boston, the "vigorous" (vig) back then was five percent on the dollar and reported to be well over one million dollars a week for the city's bullies. If you couldn't or didn't make an agreed upon payment, you were sure to have a problem. Most cases of a delinquent bill in Boston resulted in broken bones. However, in New York they did things a little different. First they intimidated you, and then they would disable your truck somehow, and then give you a beating, and if you still didn't pay, then they would just kill you. One way or another you paid the New York mob fees. Well, Buddy would have none of that and flatly refused.

Buddy told the man, "I don't pay no fee to nobody for doing my job!"

The man looked at his companions and laughed, saying, "You will, guy, one way or another."

When it was their turn, Buddy backed the truck up to the dock and started to unload the cargo without incident. When they had finished unloading Buddy waited for the load to be delivered so they could continue on their trip.

When the load finally came and Buddy was signing for it, Ryan yelled to him, "Hey, Buddy, look," pointing to the rear tires, two of which were flat. I guess the mob guy was right— they did pay a fee, the cost of a new tire. But to make matters worse they had removed the spare to hold the returning cargo, which meant they had to buy two tires. This would cost the partners the money they would have made for the entire trip, which was far from complete.

When Buddy returned home, he told Bob about Albany and how it had cost them the price of two new tires. Bob was just happy that Buddy had returned unharmed, and the truck was still in working order.

SEVEN

Buddy was now more determined to get back to Albany, but he also knew that next time there would be more trouble. Buddy wondered how they would try to stop him next time, but he got himself prepared with extra tires, four just in case. He began running different scenarios in his mind, hoping for the best outcome with the least amount of violence. Violence was always Buddy's last resort. He felt that honorable men could sit down calmly and talk out their differences, and that it was the wannabes that have to show how tough they are. And the guys from Albany had all the makings of wannabes.

For about a month Travelers Transportation had nothing going back to Albany. Finally, an order was placed, but this time it was Bob Mahoney's turn to go. However, Buddy was anticipating trouble. He insisted that he go in Bob's place. He explained to Bob that it would be better if they saw the same guy delivering, that maybe it wouldn't be as bad. A reluctant Bob was worried about the trouble and of course Buddy. He knew how Buddy felt about the Albany situation. He also knew Buddy and how no one was going to tell him what he had to do, not even the Italians. After telling Buddy how he felt to no avail, Bob finally gave in and agreed to let him go, but only if he took someone else with him. Buddy knew he was in for trouble with this run and decided to take

Ryan for his muscle and his company. Ryan was a big kid, 6'3", with blond hair and blue eyes, nineteen years old, and his boxing knowledge always made for a good ride.

So, off Buddy and his helper, Ryan, went. He figured he should bring Ryan because he was there the first time. And Ryan, remembering what had happened last trip, decided to bring along a couple of baseball bats to keep them company, just in case they were needed.

They arrived in Albany without incident and started to unload their truck. Just as last time, the local muscle, once again, approached the two men. It was the same man as before, but this time the big muscle boss man brought along three thugs to intimidate and apply some pressure to get his point across. One guy was enormous—he must have stood 6'6" tall and weighed close to 350 pounds. But Buddy didn't care. Once again, he wouldn't be pushed around in the same conversation as before about the fee and all.

Buddy told him, "Guess you didn't hear me the first time. I refuse to pay nobody anything extra for doing my job." This pissed the mob boss off.

With a smirk he said, "I guess you fellas didn't learn your lesson last time. You remember, when your tires went flat on ya! I guess you guys need a little extra incentive!" He gestured for his three henchmen to move in on the two truck drivers.

Buddy quickly intervened and shouted, "Hold it a minute!" The boss thought he was going to give in, so the three mob enforcers stopped where they stood. Buddy suggested they talk about this. He was sure they could come to some kind of agreement where everyone would be happy, and no fees would be involved. The muscle boss couldn't believe what he was hearing. With a smirk and a laugh he looked at his three henchmen and motioned for them to continue. But Buddy put his hand up a second time and said, "All right . . . this guy's just a helper (pointing to Ryan). I'll fight, but one at a time." The boss started to laugh. He was confident of his men's fighting ability, and besides, who the hell was this skinny little 5'8" baby faced Irish kid from Boston? He gestured once again, but this time just to the biggest man.

The mob boss sharply blurted out, "Get 'em," and the big guy moved in for the kill. Buddy danced around with the big guy until he got his timing down. When he did, Buddy hit him with a flurry of body shots, and while he was recovering from the blows, trying to catch his breath, he knocked him out so fast that if you blinked you would have missed it. It was one quick shot to the jaw, and it was all over—the big guy never knew what hit him. The other two men instinctively started to circle Buddy.

Ryan, seeing this, pulled out one of the bats from under his heavy coat and calmly reminded them, "One at a time, boys. You'll get your chance." With that, one of the two remaining men started toward Buddy, arms flailing. Buddy, who was barely getting warmed up, started with his body shots and then connected with the man's face and promptly knocked him out, even faster than the first guy. When the last man witnessed this, he didn't want any part of Buddy. The mob boss motioned for him to "Get 'em!" But he hesitated. After what he just witnessed with the other two men, he wasn't so anxious now! But Ryan wouldn't take "no" for an answer. He insisted by yelling, as he pounded the palm of his hand with the bat. "You wanted to fight before, when it was three on one. You're gonna fight now, pal!" The man reluctantly moved forward, and that's all Buddy McLean needed. He stepped up and gave him one good solid punch, which put the man down for the count, and out for the whole afternoon for that matter. Now, the big mob boss was left standing all alone. He was panicking; Buddy could see it in his eyes. Buddy had just knocked out three of his best men, and Ryan was standing ready with the bat in his hand. The mob Boss was, with no exaggeration, shitting his pants. Buddy calmly went over and slapped him around a bit.

He told him his name was Buddy McLean from Boston and explained to the man, "I don't pay no extra fees, and neither does any other truck driver that comes in here from Boston or anywhere from now on. They ain't gonna pay you one penny ever again, and if I hear that anybody does, I'm gonna come for you personally." Then, Buddy proceeded to knock him down to the ground. When he spun him around his arm somehow got broken. Seeing what had happened, Buddy told the man, "You won't collect any more fees with that arm, will ya, pal?" Buddy could hear a commotion going on behind him. When he turned around all the bystanders and workers on the docks started to applaud. The drivers cheered as Buddy finished loading his truck. They were finally free of paying fees, making Buddy a legend. They were finally able to pick up their loads for free. These drivers, like others, had been forced to pay the local mob extortion money for years because they needed their jobs, arms, and legs to work, but never again after that day.

EIGHT

When Buddy returned from Albany, the drivers had already heard what had happened, and the McLaughlins were not happy, once again. In the days to follow Buddy's return, the McLaughlins were beginning to lose their hold on the docks, but they still controlled a lot of the surrounding territories, including a lot of the bars and the "after hours" joints, except the few that belonged to the Italians.

Within weeks of this incident, Buddy McLean became a truck driver's hero. He had become well known up and down the entire eastern coastline and across the country. The word among the drivers had spread like wildfire through many of the truck stops across the United States. The word was out that an Irish kid from Boston, Buddy McLean, stood up to the Albany mob. No one would have to pay anything extra for taking loads out of New York ever again. Buddy became the truck driver's hero almost overnight.

Jimmy Hoffa was intrigued about the story that was circulating regarding the Irish kid from Boston taking on three Albany tough guys single-handed. This was just what the teamsters needed—access to the Albany docks. He had to meet this kid and see if he could get him into the teamsters union . . . maybe be muscle for him in the future. This was the kind of kid he needed, someone who could hold his own and who could intimidate with just a look, and Buddy could do just that!

Soon after hearing of Buddy, Jimmy reached out to his good friend Arthur O'Rourke, Secretary Treasurer of the Teamsters Local #25, to find out more about Buddy. Arthur assured Jimmy that Buddy was a good kid, that he knew the family that raised him, they were good people. Jimmy wanted to meet Buddy. This is just what the teamsters needed, an opening to New York, and to think this skinny little Irish kid from Boston did what Jimmy had been trying to do for years now.

He asked Arthur if he could get him into the Teamsters Local #25, and Arthur told him, "No problem, Jimmy, I will take care of it myself."

Jimmy said, "And Arthur, I'd like to meet him," so Arthur agreed to set up a meeting between Jimmy and Buddy. Jimmy had hoped to recruit Buddy for his own purposes; Buddy would be a welcome asset to Jimmy and the teamsters. Buddy was more than ecstatic at the idea of being a teamster, something he'd hoped and worked for, and meeting with Jimmy Hoffa himself was more than he could have asked.

After his meeting with Buddy, Jimmy was clearly impressed by this Irish kid from Boston, tough as nails with a baby face and a smile that could kill, but the eyes—that was what impressed him the most. They certainly were intimidating.

He told Buddy, "When you're ready to join the teamsters just let me know. I would be glad to have you on board." It didn't take Buddy long to decide, and he was able to get into his first union, Teamsters Local #25, thanks to Arthur O'Rourke, and his good friend Jimmy Hoffa. Jimmy also got the privilege of giving Buddy his first teamsters award for having the most hours of service in New England. Jimmy respected Buddy for his principles; he was an honest man, doing an honest job, not letting anyone stop him. Over the years Jimmy followed Buddy's accomplishments, always done without bloodshed, maybe a few black eyes, or broken bones, but never any malice in him. Buddy proved to be the kind of man most of these guys wanted to be like, a stand-up man with growing respect, and liked by everyone. However, Buddy was not someone you could take advantage of. He was much smarted than that. Jimmy knew Buddy would never work for him; he was too good of a man. But Jimmy was willing to settle for his friendship, something he was proud of.

NINE

After the incident in Albany, the McLaughlin and Hughes brothers were learning just how tough Buddy McLean really was. They tried, on a number of occasions, to recruit him as a leg breaker. But Buddy was never interested. Trying to be polite, he always refused with a smile and would change the subject, not to offend. The McLaughlins continued to try to get Buddy to join them so they could start doing business in Somerville and increase their territory but were stopped every time by Buddy's Winter Hill Gang.

Buddy and Jean were invited to several different parties the McLaughlins had at the Alibi Lounge. The Alibi was the only place that had live entertainment back in those days. Buddy introduced Jean to two of the McLaughlin brothers, Bernie and George. Georgie was only a little shit, smaller than Jean. Bernie was taller but still a little shit. The few times when Buddy and Jean were there they couldn't pay for anything. They always tried to make Buddy and Jean feel comfortable, making a big deal over them, giving them the best seats, and waiting on them hand and foot. Having Buddy on their crew as an enforcer would make the McLaughlins invincible. With Buddy's contacts and the respect he had earned among the teamsters and longshoremen, they would control the whole eastern seaboard. However, Buddy would have nothing to do with the brothers or their plans. He had his own plans, and they were to keep them and their pals off the docks forever.

TEN

One night Buddy and his good friend Russell Nickerson, a metropolitan police officer, went up to a popular Charlestown night spot, the Stork Club, for a drink. Now this was a place the McLaughlin brothers loved to go and drink, as did their henchmen, Connie and Stevie Hughes. Buddy and Russ joined some others friends from Somerville who were having drinks, minding their own business. The Charlestown crowd consisted of Dickey Crowley, a Boston cop and good friend of the McLaughlins; Gene Cook, a onetime McLaughlin loan shark and leg breaker; Jim Lombardo; Richard "Ditso" Doherty; and "Juney" Raso. They were all in a booth having a drink. A so-called friend of Buddy's by the name of Sal Macerelli (a "friend" of Buddy's who didn't help once the gang war started) had a few words with Gene Cook, who was sitting at the Charlestown crew's table. Without warning, all hell broke loose. Gene cold cocked Sal, and then Jim Lombardo stood up and hit anyone in his reach. Buddy did the same. It became a free for all. Punches were being thrown left and right. When all was said and done the place was in total chaos, and the fight seemed to go on for hours, but it took only several minutes to destroy the joint.

Juney Raso claims, "I was knocked down so much I thought someone was turning the lights on and off." While on the floor a Somerville guy lay beside him, Buddy McLean, who was trying to get to his feet and regain his composure. So Juney, in defense of his home town, lashed out with the heel of his foot at the man, his foot connecting to his face, kicking out Buddy McLean's two front teeth. In all the confusion, when Buddy looked up to see who had kicked him, it was Ditso Doherty's face he saw. Buddy started to get up once again when a surge of Charlestown guys came rushing in. This seemed to go on forever, but Somerville was holding its own. While the other men were fighting, Buddy was on the floor looking for his teeth. Buddy eventually found his pearly whites, which he snatched up from the Stork Club floor and quickly put in his pocket.

Buddy was irate about his teeth, which hurt like hell, and he wanted revenge, an eye for an eye and a few teeth for a few teeth. Buddy insisted that a kid by the name of Ditso Doherty was responsible and wanted another crack at the guy. It would be almost a month before Buddy would get his chance. Buddy McLean was a stand-up fighter who never liked dirty fighters. If he knocked someone to the ground, he would give them a chance to get to their feet before he would throw his next punch, but most of the time they couldn't or wouldn't get up, so they stayed down. By this time Buddy had a pretty good reputation as a tough guy. He had beaten Herby Bolduc, a former U.S. Navy heavyweight champ and New England heavyweight champ. The two fought behind a lumber yard in Charlestown. As usual, Buddy was sticking up for one of his friends, whom Bolduc had done a number on. Buddy beat Bolduc by wearing him down with his quick and accurate body blows. Bolduc would prove to be his "toughest fight ever," according to the man himself. Buddy also won a number of brawls down at the Alibi Bar in Charlestown.

Buddy remembered the fight he had with Joseph "Joker" McDonald, a bartender-bouncer and middleweight pro fighter, who had an argument with Buddy over Chinese food the bar was serving. Joker McDonald, like so many others, fought in vain that night as a tougher Buddy beat him ferociously to end the fight quickly. After the fight Buddy was going to the men's room to freshen up when another tough guy by the name of Bobby Stafford jumped him from behind. Stafford had the initial advantage but also lost. Buddy was warmed up and beat him so quickly that Bobby never got to throw a punch.

Stafford never did, but Joe "Joker" McDonald ended up liking Buddy and even worked at the 318 (a.k.a. Pal Joey's) and the Capital Café, both atop Winter Hill in Somerville.

After the Stork Club incident and two missing teeth, Buddy went to see his dentist on Broadway. The doctor was a great dentist whom Buddy liked, and through a series of visits he was able to re-root Buddy's two front teeth. This was unheard of at the time and cost Buddy a lot of money. The doctor's unique work took weeks to finish but was well worth the wait. He also made him a mouth guard to protect the new pearly whites, which Buddy always carried with him.

Jean joked during this time, saying, "All Buddy wanted for Christmas was his two front teeth."

Just a few days after the Stork Club incident, with his two teeth missing, Buddy went down to the Mystic Bridge Café in City Square, Charlestown. It was the main hangout for the McLaughlin crew. It was owned by McLaughlin muscle Stevie Hughes Jr. Buddy went in like a gentleman. He left word with the McLaughlin crew that he wanted to fight the man he felt responsible for kicking out his two front teeth.

The Charlestown crew sent a messenger to the Capitol one week later regarding Buddy's request for the rematch. Seemed the McLaughlin brothers wanted to turn this thing into an all-out gang brawl. Word was out they all wanted rematches. Although Buddy's friends would have liked nothing better, he sent word back to Charlestown that there would only be one fight, between him and Ditso Doherty. He told the McLaughlins this wasn't going to turn into a gang fight either: "It's just him and me, one on one, no outsiders." The response was favorable to Buddy McLean's request for a rematch with Ditso Doherty.

ELEVEN

The McLaughlins had never seen Buddy fight before but had heard about his fighting ability. Buddy was gaining popularity at the local watering holes controlled by the McLaughlins in Charlestown, including the Alibi. Buddy had a good name in Charlestown. He was well liked, people knew he was a stand-up guy, and people were really starting to look up to him, which started to worry the brothers—it also worried Buddy. He knew the brothers were dangerous, all of them.

Bernard "Bernie" McLaughlin, born in 1921, had a criminal record that began at the ripe age of eleven with breaking windows. He soon expanded his record to larceny and was sent to the Shirley Massachusetts Reform School in 1938. After a few more minor brushes with the law, he was charged with assault and battery and attempted robbery from an August 21, 1947 incident involving Boston City Councilman John A. Winkler. McLaughlin was ultimately wounded by a patrolman as he attempted to flee the scene. He was acquitted for the original charges of assault and battery and robbery. Bernie was picked up for several public drunkenness charges in 1949–1950 and twice on bookmaking charges in 1955.

Brother Edward "Punchy" McLaughlin, born in 1917, was the oldest of the three, and their muscle. Punchy was also an ex-Merchant Marine, occasional longshoreman, a former pro boxer, and an aide (bodyguard) to former Massachusetts Governor Peabody. He also eventually became a labor organizer for the Merchant Marine union. Punchy had numerous incidents with the law but had only a mild criminal record compared to his brother Bernie. Punchy was fined $500 for stealing a TV set in Lynn in 1958. That same year he was fined a hundred dollars for shoplifting a pair of pantyhose. His career as a criminal began earlier than Bernie's—at the age of nine he was picked up for larceny, and by thirteen he was judged a stubborn child and then sent off to the rigid Lyman Reform School. Although he was never imprisoned again he had thirty-eight entries on his police arrest record. Punchy was also believed to have received a piece of the famous 1.5 million dollar Plymouth Mail Heist. Rumor has it he did this by shaking down the actual robbers for his fee, which was rightfully his. This however was a rumor, probably spread by him.

Finally there was George McLaughlin. No one knows exactly what George's role was in the McLaughlins' businesses. He was a member of the United States Navy, which certified him as a psychopath with psychopathic tendencies. George was ultimately given a Bad Conduct Discharge. He also had a lengthy police record stemming from as early as 1948, when his assault with intent to murder would land him in jail. He was sentenced to five years and a day, at the correctional institution in Concord, Massachusetts. Also a part-time longshoreman, Georgie had a reputation for sporadic and spontaneous action. He was known to be extremely unpredictable and dangerous. George's record also includes three assault and batteries, armed assault with intent to rob, suspicion of armed assault, and armed robbery. In 1964

George made the FBI's Ten Most Wanted List for the cold-blooded murder of William Sheridan, a twenty-one-year-old bank clerk. When George was finally captured and taken off the streets during the tail end of the war, he was immediately placed in police custody.

The McLaughlin brothers had their own bookmaking and loansharking operation mixed with many other illegal activities. They also required a percentage of any illegal action taking place within their territory. This was all approved and cleared by one or more of the Five Families, to whom the McLaughlin brothers paid homage directly.

Assisting the McLaughlin brothers were their childhood friends, the Hughes brothers, Connie and Stevie. Just like the three McLaughlins, both of the Hughes brothers were feared throughout the docks and the entire waterfront up and down the eastern seaboard.

Stevie, the older of the two, born in 1927, had an extensive violent criminal past just like his bosses. He was referred to by police as a "social menace." The 6'3", 235-pounder also worked as a longshoreman and in the carpenters union. He had been picked up for various offenses, such as assault and battery with intent to rob City Councilor John B. Winkler, and for the 1957 murder of former boxer and union worker Tommy Sullivan. Stevie Hughes was questioned on both of these offenses alongside his boss Bernie McLaughlin.

Born in 1929, Connie was sent to Lyman Reform School as a juvenile, during which he staged an escape. At the age of eighteen he received a five to seven year prison term for assault with a dangerous weapon. He was paroled in 1952 and was questioned on various other crimes, such as shoplifting, assault with intent to murder, armed robbery, illegal possession of drugs, and violation of the firearms law.

Buddy knew after the fight, no matter how it ended, he would have to take care of things. Buddy knew his power was growing silently, and the McLaughlins and Hughes brothers were beginning to notice.

The brothers tried every trick in the book to get Buddy on their side, but Buddy was smarter than that. When approached by Bernie to come work for them, Buddy flatly refused. Buddy was just a regular blue-collar, working-class stiff. He had a pregnant wife and three small children at the time. He didn't want anything to do with a life of crime or any of those thugs. It had been hard enough dealing with the thugs from New York, and he didn't want to have to do it at home.

Buddy knew he would someday have his run-ins with the brothers of both families, as they were starting to get itchy over who controlled what. And with the Italians to contend with as well, he knew he had to figure out how to keep the brothers at bay and not to offend the Italians. He would have to have a sit-down with the powers that be.

TWELVE

Bill McLean, who was also a longshoreman and a checker on the waterfront, was told by a friend about a fight about to happen with his son, Buddy, and Joe DeAngeles in Charlestown. Bill McLean wasn't nervous about Buddy fighting. He was nervous about him fighting a fight in Charlestown, a legitimate concern, and he had the last man to beat Rocky Marciano to beat Joe DeAngeles.

The fight with Joe lasted only three minutes. Buddy had his timing down in two, with a few body blows, then a quick right to the chin, and it was all over. A few mornings later on their way to work, Buddy told Ryan they we're going to make a quick stop on the way in. Buddy, while giving him directions, told him about the fight he had with Joe DeAngeles. Buddy explained to him how he was down at the Alibi lounge and had a fight with the great Joe DeAngeles. The word was Buddy had knocked him out cold. Now after everything got straightened out that night, or so he thought: Unbeknownst to him, Joe, trying not to lose face, was going around saying, "I was drunk! That's the only reason Buddy McLean beat me, 'cause I was drunk. If I wasn't I would have creamed that kid."

Buddy motions Ryan to stop at this house, and Buddy gets out of the car and goes up the stairs and rings the bell. Out comes Joe DeAngeles. He sees Buddy and he almost shits himself.

40

Buddy says, "Take it easy, Joe! I heard you made the statement you were drunk when we fought. Well I want to give you a chance to redeem yourself! So step outside right now, and we can have it out again, unless you're still drunk!"

Joe says, "Look, Buddy, I've had enough of you. I don't want no part of ya. I'd rather be friends with ya."

Buddy told him he had wanted it to be a fair fight that night, and at the time, he thought it was, and he didn't like the drunk story Joe was telling. Buddy didn't want people to think he would take advantage of someone who was drunk, as it was not his style.

Buddy told him, "Only under one condition—you have to start telling people the truth about the beating, 'cause if you don't I will have to come back and defend my reputation." Joe agreed never to tell the story again because he didn't want a return visit from him. Buddy came down the stairs and got in the car and told Ryan, "I don't think we will hear any more stories from that guy," pointing up toward Joe's house. Just by the look in Buddy's eyes and the tone of his voice Ryan knew this to be true. The two men went off to work in silence.

Things began to intensify with the brothers of Charlestown as to who was the toughest. They decided to end this once and for all. They wanted to beat the shit out of Buddy, to put him in his place and show him they ran things around the docks. So they agreed to the one-on-one so Buddy could get his revenge with Ditso. It would be just the two of them, or so they would make it seem.

THIRTEEN

Before the fight a good friend of Buddy's, Al, who knew Buddy would beat Ditso, tried to reason with the Charlestown youth and get Ditso to back out. Even though Ditso was a good fighter and a good kid, he wasn't really with the McLaughlins. They were just using him to get at Buddy, who was gaining popularity, attention, and a reputation as a great fighter, unbeatable.

The brothers never saw him fight and wanted to test the waters with Buddy, to see how tough he really was. Ditso told Al that he wasn't the one who kicked Buddy in the mouth, knocking out his two front teeth. Knowing what kind of kid Ditso was, he knew he wouldn't lie about this, so he believed him when he told him it was Juney Raso. He asked Ditso to let him explain this to Buddy. He told him Buddy would understand.

Ditso refused, saying, "No thanks, Al. He thinks I kicked him, so I'll fight him. Let it alone." Ditso wasn't trying to be a tough guy, but he wasn't about to rat on his friend Juney Raso, who had really done the deed. "If you tell Buddy that it wasn't me, I'll look like a coward, and I don't want people to think I am. I have to live here." Al understood.

"Okay, kid, if that's the way you want it, fine with me, but Buddy's fucking tough, Ditso. You're good, but I'm telling you, this guy's fucking scary. Just do me one favor. If you're gonna fight him, fight him 'clean.' He'll fight by whatever rules you set down, so tell him you want a clean fight, no hitting while your opponent is on the ground. Whoever doesn't get up is the loser. Tell him no kicking whatsoever, and he'll go along with that, but he's still gonna beat ya, and by your own rules." Ditso agreed to let the fight go on as planned.

A few nights later in Coleman's bar on lower Broadway, Buddy came walking in and saw his friend Al.

Buddy said, "Hey, Al, how ya doing?"

"Fine, Buddy, but can I have a word with you?" Al asked.

"Sure," Buddy said. So Al pulled Buddy aside to explain to him how Ditso wasn't a bad kid. He wasn't like the other guys down at the Stork Club. He told Buddy. He got trapped into this thing defending his friends.

"He ain't a dirty kid. He ain't a fuckin thief, or no fuckin gangster, but he's a tough kid."

Buddy said, "I heard that he's a real tough fighter."

"Yes, he is," Al told him. "He's tough, but if you take him in the fucking ring he might win on points. In a clean fight, who knows!" The news Al had given him about Ditso seemed to fall on deaf ears. All Buddy knew was that Ditso was a dirty fighter, kicking him like a girl.

John Hurley was already down at the field checking out things for Buddy, even though he was neutral at this time, waiting for the rest of the crew to arrive. Meanwhile, Buddy and his "friends" met at Charlie's Grill. By the time the rest of their crew had arrived, the spectators from the Charlestown side had grown to an incredible number. Without exaggeration, there had to be well over two hundred people there. Once there, the Somerville crowd all stayed close together. The Charlestown crowd was all scattered around the field, which gave you an uneasy feeling.

The McLaughlin crew was standing firm at the twenty-five-yard line on the south side of the field. The Somerville crowd gathered on the twenty-five-yard line on the north side. The Somerville men had good positioning, with their backs to a fence adjacent to the Metro Coal Co. building. We had just started to say hello to some of the Somerville guys who were there, when a young kid by the name of "Pudgy" O'Conner came running up.

Pudgy was yet another talented boxer from Charlestown, who was sparring partners for Cannen Basillio, Paul Pender, among other greats. However, his family refused to give him their blessing, and he never turned pro. Pudgy came running over to Buddy Cochran and John. He was very excited. He thought there might be a big gang fight with the McLaughlins and Hugheses against The Winter Hill gang, so he was all wound up. Out of breath he managed to put a sentence together.

He said, "Oh Jesus! Am I glad you guys are here. You're gonna need everybody you got. The McLaughlin brothers got a shit load of guns down there on the field, so many it ain't funny." Now, this was just thirty minutes before the big fight. So Buddy Cochran and John took a look around, and by now there must have been three to four hundred people on or around the field. John knew Buddy Cochran and his boys were there for Buddy and that they would be ready if this turned nasty.

John told him, "Get over there with the rest of the Somerville people and don't talk to nobody 'til Buddy and Uncle Joe Mac (McDonald) show up! Keep your mouths shut and your eyes and ears open! I'll wait here for Uncle Joe and Buddy. When they finally get here I'll tell them of the situation—how the McLaughlins and Hugheses have several guns hanging around the field and there's a good chance they're gonna kill Buddy if he wins!"

When they arrived John told them of the events. He probably should have just told Joe this, but he wanted Buddy to be aware. It didn't matter anyhow; the news didn't seem to faze either one of them. John found out after the fight that just around the corner Joe McDonald had his own stash of guns just waiting for the signal. Joe McDonald was no fool—he was ready for anything.

"Don't worry, John," Joe said. "I have things under control. It's Buddy fighting . . . did you think he would come here alone? You'd be surprised as to who is here to help Buddy, if it comes to that."

The word spread. As the time approached, the field began to fill up on both sides. It was incredible—so many people from different cities just to see this fight. Joe was prepared with his cars loaded with muscle and firearms, waiting within eyesight, just in case they were needed. A circle was made for them to fight in, and they were both awaiting the rules.

Buddy was wearing a sweatshirt with the sleeves cut off, a pair of chino pants, and a mouth piece to protect his new teeth. Buddy was told to and did stand close to Joe McDonald. Across the way standing ready was Ditso Doherty. He was wearing chinos and a green T-shirt. He was standing beside all of the heavies—Bernie McLaughlin, Punchy McLaughlin, Steven "Old Man" Hughes, Sr., father to Stevie and Connie Hughes. All were present and accounted for just as the Hill expected. The word got back to the Hill that after the fight was over, Old Man Hughes (considered the most dangerous of all of them) was going to take out Joe McDonald should anything go wrong.

FOURTEEN

Joseph Maurice McDonald, another union man, Teamsters Local #25. Joe was a former Navy war hero during WWII. In August 1942, while aboard his last ship, the USS *Quincy*, with his brother Jackie, Joe learned that Jackie was reported missing in action after their ship was torpedoed and sunk at Guadalcanal. Joe swam around in shark infested waters with the ship's depth charges going off all around him looking for his brother. Needless to say, Jackie's body was never recovered. Joseph McDonald was also a former Golden Gloves champion, born and raised on Golden Ave. in Medford.

Joe was known to many as a great guy who extended loans and favors to friends. During the holiday season, he and Buddy would bring fruit baskets and ten-pound turkeys or hams to many needy families in Somerville. Joe's good heart and warm nature helped feed many children who might have gone hungry. On the other hand, Joe was described as a "murderous, psychopathic bank robber," in a book written by a former Somerville police officer, Billy B. Breen, who was also responsible for trying to frame Joe McDonald for a bank robbery in Tampa, Florida. Joe was merely an intelligent man with a very high IQ. He won the case anyway.

"Uncle Joe," as he was known up on Winter Hill, was well liked and loved by many. Anyone who knew the real

Joseph Maurice McDonald knew a man with a heart of gold, but cross him, and he would have yours on a plate, literally. If he ever used the word "Mista" you were in serious trouble. On the other hand he was very thoughtful. If you were in an accident, Uncle Joe would give you a kidney, or his liver. That was if he liked you, but if you fucked with him . . . he would just kill you.

Joe McDonald was one of the few men that the McLaughlin and Hughes brothers both respected and feared. Joe owned a lot of property up on Winter Hill and had lots of interests in other cities. He lived on Marshall St. in Somerville for a while, where he ran the Hill. Joe McDonald was the beginning of Somerville. This heavily populated, blue-collar, working-class city was a loan shark's playground. And Joe did play.

Joe had another brother, Leo McDonald. Like his younger brother, Leo was also a reputed bank robber. He had a similar temperament and was considered capable but not quite as vicious as Joe. Joe and his brother, Leo, were arrested on January 20, 1960. The two brothers were arrested in connection with a robbery that had taken place at the Sunny Hurst Dairy in Stoneham. To this day, Joe swears, even to his closest of friends on the Hill, he wasn't there that day. But he was arrested and convicted just the same. Witnesses say that two masked bandits entered the dairy through a rear door that had been left unlocked in expectation of a dairy transport truck. One of the masked men stuck a gun to the back of the plant engineer's, Robert Kerwin's, head and forced Kerwin to lead them through a maze of equipment and a series of tunnels to the front of the building. Once there, they forced another worker, Edward May, to hand over two days' worth of receipts. All the while, the seven other people were told to remain still with their hands in the air. Unknown to the gunmen, a nine-year-old boy, the son of the manager, was hiding a packet of ten dollar bills behind his back. A third stick-up man stood ready, gun in hand, in the outer hallway while his two accomplices looted the cash register. The getaway car was a red and white sedan stolen from Charlestown just hours before. Although the gunmen were masked and made a clean getaway with $13,200 in cash and checks, four of the victims could pick out the robbers from photographs due to "red hair" and "crossed eyes." Leo McDonald of Somerville was identified, arrested and held. Leo spent most of his time in jail during the gang war, or he would have been a great help.

Another bigwig who attended the "Big Fight" was Gabriel "Old Man" Grande, who had a son named Raymond. "Young" Raymond Grande chummed around with Buddy and the other Winter Hill Gang members. While Old Man Grande served as a mentor for Buddy and Joe McDonald during the gang war, he gave the two men a lot of good, sound advice. He provided essential information during the war; he obtained much of this through his Italian connections in Boston and Rhode Island. The communication with the Italians was essential during the war. Without Buddy's and Old Man Grande's connections, the war could have gone on much longer.

FIFTEEN

Old Man Hughes had a bad reputation and was considered the worst of them all up on the Hill. He was the most ruthless and heartless of them all; he never took pity on anyone. You crossed his path, and you would usually end up dead or close to it. With his two sons, Old Man Hughes was able to control most of Charlestown.

In the stands were all Charlestown locals, many of whom were hoping this would turn into a big free-for-all, and God knows the odds were on their side that day. The eight Charlestown heavies made the first move. They walked out a little ways and stopped. Ditso continued on alone to the fifty-yard line. At the same time Buddy and Joe Mac followed suit and made their way out. Joe and Buddy met Ditso alone at the fifty-yard line. Buddy spoke first.

"What rules do you want to do this by?"

Ditso said, "Whatever you want!"

Buddy answered, "Anything goes . . . but no kicking!" Ditso agreed, and the two started to circle each other. There were no referees. Joe DeAngeles, who everyone thought would referee, never showed up. This was thought to be just a rumor spread by the McLaughlins to try to intimidate Buddy.

Ditso and Buddy squared up and started to circle each other at the fifty-yard line. Buddy was in his unorthodox fighter's stance, with his hands held high and his elbows tucked in. His lips were protruding from the mouth piece he used to protect his new pearly whites, and his fists were constantly moving to throw off his opponent's timing. The crowd's intensity grew as everyone waited for the first punch to be thrown. As it happened, Ditso struck first. He got in a few quick jabs, a hook and a couple of rights. He landed about five to six good, clean punches. The Charlestown crowd was going crazy. So were the Hugheses and McLaughlins, but Old Man Hughes was a little more subtle. The Hill later learned that the McLaughlins had taken out some big action on Ditso that day. This meant they weren't planning on a loss. One way or the other, they would win.

Buddy took a few shots but was just getting warmed up as he was starting to get Ditso's timing down. If you were scoring the fight, Ditso won the first round. Each time he hit Buddy, the Charlestown crowd went wild. Then, Buddy started in on him with body shots. Ditso would hit high, and Buddy would kiss his kidneys and his rib area. The more Ditso punched up high, the more Buddy would rip him with body blows. Then, Buddy started to pound him on the forearms. Slowly but surely they started to come down by his side, thus leaving Ditso's face wide open. It didn't take Buddy long to capitalize on that. This had been the way Buddy won most of his fights, body blows and kidney kisses, wearing them down for the kill. He with his everlasting stamina could also take the punches that would eventually wear down his opponents.

Finally, Ditso couldn't hold his arms up any longer. They were way down by his side at this point. Buddy, seeing his opening, hit him with a right and connected with his jaw, which dropped him. The Charlestown side went quiet. The Somerville side let out a cheer for their fighter, but it wasn't in a mocking manor. Buddy's supporters were still well aware of the overwhelming odds, so they strained not to get too caught up in the moment. Ditso was down but in good shape for this fight. He got up quickly and came right back after Buddy. Buddy had sidestepped him and again hit him with another right. This one spun him completely around, then back to the ground. Ditso got up once again, but this time a lot slower. Rising to one knee first, trying to clear his head, shaking it, finally getting to his feet, he charged Buddy before Buddy could pound him with another outrageous attack. He charged Buddy, and the two ended up in a clinch. They wrestled to the ground, but the rules still weren't broken. Ditso had Buddy in a headlock and, from the reaction on Buddy's face, probably threw dirt in his face. Ditso started to hammer away on Buddy's head and ear. Once again the silent Charlestown crowd was heard again. Buddy broke the headlock and got up off the ground faster than Ditso could. Buddy, giving Ditso time to clear his head again and regain his composure, went right at him with his quick right uppercut, and down Ditso went out cold, with a couple of his teeth missing to boot. And now that Buddy felt he had evened the score, the fight was over. Or that's what Buddy thought. Buddy had gotten what he wanted—"a few teeth for a few teeth."

But Big Butchie Quinn, a Charlestown native and a Navy heavyweight boxer, was home on furlough watching the big fight that day. Butchie was approximately 6'4" and 230 pounds. He was a loyal Charlestown man, willing to fight for his town. Ditso was still down when Butchie came running out onto the field.

He yelled over to Buddy, "Hey, Somerville tough guy, try someone your own size, like me!"

Buddy replied, "Who the hell are you?"

Butchie answered, "I'm a townie, and I want a piece of ya! Try me on for size!"

With that, Joe McDonald turned to John Hurley and asked, "Who the fuck is he? Is he one of their guns?"

John answered quickly, "No, Uncle Joe, he's just a sailor home on leave. Let him go." Otherwise, Joe would have intervened and stopped it before it started.

Buddy moved closer to a much bigger Butchie Quinn and said, "Hey, pal, I got no beef with you. You probably don't even know how this fight started." Butchie looked at Buddy and slowly spoke.

"Like I said, you're bigger than him, and I'm a townie! It's my turn. I want a piece of ya!" Buddy wasn't that much bigger than Ditso. He maybe had twenty pounds on the guy. But this guy must have been sixty to seventy pounds heavier and a good five to six inches taller than Buddy. Many people thought Buddy was already tired from the first fight, but little did they know he was just getting warmed up. Although Buddy didn't have a beef with this guy, he couldn't back down now—he had to finish it, and he would. Buddy looked to Joe Mac, who slowly stepped out of the crowd.

He gave Buddy a nod of approval and quietly said, "Go for it, Buddy."

Then, he looked over to the Charlestown crowd and yelled, "But this ends it! Nobody else!" Buddy made it clear to everyone that this was the last fight. No one else was going to butt in, or there would be trouble. Buddy turned to Quinn and said, "Okay, fella, let's go!" Butchie had no idea how Buddy fought.

Quinn was wearing a white T-shirt and his Navy white bell bottom pants. He took off his T-shirt to intimidate the smaller Buddy, who looked at Quinn and mumbled, "Holy shit—this guy's huge!" The two started to circle each other. Buddy landed the first couple of jabs. But to each one of Buddy's, Quinn threw and landed five or six of his own. The Charlestown people were really going crazy now. Same as the last fight, Quinn got the better of Buddy in the beginning as it seemed. This guy was powerful. But it didn't take long for Buddy to get Quinn's timing down, so he started with the body blows. He started to rip away at Quinn's middle, then kidney section, and with each punch you could see him lifting Quinn off the ground. Buddy just kept firing away, with blind determination. He started to beat down this mountain of a man.

Quinn was starting to get tired. He had to go for the knockout. He moved in trying to go for the kill, one quick knockout punch. Quinn's arms were low at this point, and Buddy took notice. Before Quinn could throw one more punch, Buddy threw a few knockout punches of his own. Buddy threw three hard blows to Butchie's face. The punches were so hard that Buddy knocked him out for even longer than Ditso, who was still being attended to by the five brothers. Quinn was so still the Somerville men thought Buddy had killed him. Everyone on the field thought for sure he was dead. This quieted the Charlestown crowd once and for all. Even though the crowd was for the Charlestown fighters, most of them hated the five brothers anyway. After a while they went to see whether poor Butchie was even breathing. He was alright and finally got up and left the field unassisted, but Buddy had cut his face up pretty good. And as far as Ditso was concerned, the fight was over. Eventually, they called an ambulance for him because he was still on the ground long after Quinn got up and left. The brothers didn't want to move him. But he did survive the battle with a few cuts and lots of bruises, and don't forget minus his two front teeth.

A deranged thug from Charlestown came running toward Buddy screaming, "I'll knock him out, the little shit." Buddy stood waiting for his first blow to be thrown when the thug swung and missed, giving Buddy the opportunity to land a perfect uppercut, and down he went. The kid was one of McLaughlin's thugs who wanted to keep the fight going. But the Charlestown crew and all the brothers were all standing huddled together, all mumbling something. Joe Mac and the Somerville crew stood by, ready. All of a sudden Frankie, a mouthpiece for the brothers, came running out of the crowd. Everybody thought he might be foolish enough to try to fight Buddy himself.

But instead, to everyone's surprise, he yelled out, "That's it. Nobody's gonna fight no more! It's OVER!" So Joe McDonald passed the word to the Somerville crowd. Everyone stayed still. Nobody left until he said so, and then they would all leave together.

Old Man Hughes yelled to Frankie, "Why don't you fight him?" Frankie was tough but not stupid. He wanted no part of Buddy McLean.

He told Old Man Hughes, "No! Enough's enough!"

Old Man Hughes took a step out of the Charlestown crowd, looked to Joe McDonald, and replied, "Okay, Joe, just one of those things. But I WILL see you later." Old Man Hughes made an about-face and was the first to walk off the field. He was followed by his two sons, the McLaughlin brothers, and approximately thirty to forty of their armed henchmen. Joe and Old Man Hughes had been feuding since they were kids, but that's another story.

Joe had a suit jacket on that day, so you knew he was on the ready in case Old Man Hughes tried any funny stuff. Joe certainly didn't trust his old adversary. Leo McDonald, who was also dressed and ready for the occasion, stood beside his brother, for he feared Old Man Hughes would start something. After the Charlestown crew had gone, only then did Joe give the signal for the outnumbered Somerville crowd to make their way back home. As Buddy walked to his car, he was hoping this would bring a new perspective to all the brothers. You stay in your territory, and we will stay in all of ours. Hopefully, he had taken them down a peg. And maybe he wouldn't have to fight as much. The rest of the gang went straight to their cars with not much celebration, and back to the Hill they went. After all the hand shaking and cheering Buddy headed home to get cleaned up, but the revelries went on for hours after he had left. Buddy was proud of himself, for he had confirmed to the brothers he was a force to be reckoned with and was unbeatable.

SIXTEEN

Word of the big fight had spread. It was all over the Waterfront, Charlestown, the North End, the South End, East Boston, and Downtown Boston, even as far out as Worcester and Providence, Rhode Island. The word was out—Buddy McLean was without a doubt "the toughest man in New England" again, making him a legend.

The stories that circulated after that day gave Buddy new respect. The Hughes brothers couldn't believe he knocked out two guys without breaking a sweat—only after the third guy did they see small beads of sweat on Buddy's forehead. If the words fight and Buddy McLean were used in the same sentence, everyone listened. He had never instigated a fight in his life, and he never lost one either. He prided himself on being a clean fighter and despised any dirty fighting. This would only make the beating he would give worse.

When he came home that day, my mother was there to help clean his wounds. She was telling him to stop all this fighting, and he told her that hopefully after today he wouldn't have to fight anymore. As she wiped the blood from his lip she tried to believe him, even as she put the ice on his eye. He insisted this was the end of the fighting.

I heard Dad's voice in the kitchen and got all excited thinking we might be going on the truck, and I ran in the kitchen and excitedly yelled, "Are we going on the truck today, Dad!"

"No, Michael," he said sadly. "Not today."

I could see the wounds my mother was taking care of and understood.

"Maybe next week, Michael, okay?"

"Okay, Dad, next week!"

I had seen my Dad come home like that before, and I had heard the stories of why. Seemed he was always standing up for his friends or just the little guy who couldn't defend himself. Listening to those stories always made me proud of my dad, and my mom, who, even though she knew how good a fighter her husband was, was still worried. I hadn't seen my dad that mad since the day I got the toy rifle for my birthday. He was furious. I was only four and could hardly hold the thing up, never mind shoot it.

Buddy never considered getting into business with any of those guys even though he was respected and very close with the highest of them.

Working on the docks became a challenge for Buddy after the fight, as they were McLaughlin and Italian run. But if you knew the hiring guy and paid a kickback, you would get hired for the day. Buddy didn't like this, but there wasn't much he could do about it, yet. He had his dad's union card, but the guys vying for a day's work had to feed their families, and they were the ones suffering.

Jobs were not plentiful for non-union members, so they were forced to get loans from the brothers or the Italians. When paying the loans became a problem, the brothers or the Italians would then be forced to bring bodily harm to these non-paying workers, breaking arms or legs, whichever they felt like doing that day.

On one occasion an Irish union member who had nine children couldn't pay his loan and was told they would break a leg if he didn't pay, and he replied, "Then how would I ever pay you? I wouldn't be able to work." Two days later, when the man couldn't pay, a leg was broken. When Buddy heard of this he tried to find the worker. When he did, he saw that he had no broken leg so, as usual, the story had gotten out of control, probably by the brothers to instill fear in the other borrowing drivers on the docks just as an example.

Annoyed by this, Buddy approached the man and asked "How did you pay them?"

The man replied, "I couldn't, Buddy. You know how scarce the work has been."

"But," Buddy asked. "I thought they said they would break a leg?"

"They did," he said. "They broke my eight-year-old daughter's leg." Buddy could hardly contain himself. Infuriated about the events that had just taken place, he knew something had to be done. He thought the brothers and the Italians had more class than to start hurting children. Even though he had his own lucrative hijacking schemes going on and really didn't need the money, it still bothered Buddy that the other hard working men were being taken advantage of like this.

This weighed so heavy on his mind that he decided to go to the North End and let the Italians know exactly what was going on down on the docks, between his men and the McLaughlin brothers. He wasn't sure he was ready for another beating, if it came to that, seeing as it had only been a few days since the big fight. But Buddy knew the Italians had to be told, like it or not.

SEVENTEEN

B old as he was, Buddy, having no fear, walked right into the office of Jerry Anguilo. No fear in his eyes and no weapon. Buddy was determined to let Jerry and the other Italians know that this was not how you do business, just as he told them in Albany. He was going to tell Jerry just how he felt, and as I said, there was no fear in his eyes, just blind determination. The fury he felt about what had been done was eating at him—children, who hurts children? Someone had to stand up for the struggling Irish longshoremen who were just trying to make a decent living and always willing to work as hard as they had to in order to do it.

Gennaro "Jerry" Anguilo had his connections with the Five Families (la Cosa Nostra) of New York. Like Buddy, he boldly approached Joe Lombardo and basically made him an offer he couldn't refuse. This offer kept Lombardo involved with twenty-five percent on the dollar of the daily street numbers money. Joe Lombardo accepted, and that was how Jerry took over the North End. At the same time three brothers from Charlestown, the McLaughlin brothers, had been dominating all of the Irish communities and Boston's entire waterfront. With Lombardo taking a break, they saw the opportunity to move in on the territory. The McLaughlins had seen the Italians were having trouble recruiting dedicated young men, while the Irish from the north and south sides of Boston were growing. And Buddy McLean's Winter Hill Gang was growing in popularity and was feared up and down the east coast, and anywhere a teamster went, to say you belonged to the gang instantly raised your status in the crowd. They all had their stories of how the King did this, or he beat the shit out of this one, or that one—some of these stories were very true; however, many were not.

Buddy, bold as can be, looked Jerry right in the eyes and said, "We need to talk man-to-man. This shit on the docks has to stop." Buddy proceeded to tell Jerry how the McLaughlins and his own men were handling business on the docks. Jerry was unaware of what had happened regarding the girl's leg. He was appalled, telling Buddy they had more class than to hurt a man's children. It must have been the McLaughlins, he thought. His men weren't animals and wouldn't hurt a little girl; however, the brothers would crucify their own mother if they would gain by it. When their conversation was done, Jerry agreed that he would keep his men at bay and see what he could do to help get the McLaughlins off the docks. He also told the Irish longshoreman that if he needed help to come to him—he would help. Jerry instantly liked and admired Buddy. He had balls (just as Jerry did, back in the day). He respected him for just barging in and blurting out what he had to say. No one was going to stop him. Jerry liked that about Buddy. He respected him. Jerry had heard of Buddy with all the talk of the big fight and all. The bottom line after meeting with him was that he liked the guy. Jerry also knew that word of that fight had gotten all the way to Rhode Island, to Patriaca himself.

Ray commented to him, "I like that Irish kid. He has balls. I want to meet him someday Jerry. He's a good man, I hear." Ray told Jerry, "If he comes to you for help, help him!

I'll back you." This was before the meeting. Jerry knew how Ray felt about Buddy. He respected him and knew he had the kind of power he had hoped to have someday. Ray knew this young Irish kid from the streets of Somerville, who now controlled more territories than he even knew, had more loyalty in his own town than Ray had in his whole state.

As soon as Buddy left his office, Jerry called Ray immediately and told him what had happened on the docks, and how Buddy McLean had just left his office.

Ray was very impressed, saying, "I told you he had balls. Set up a meeting with him, Jerry, now!"

Two weeks had passed since Buddy visited Jerry's office when he got word that Jerry wanted another sit-down, with only Buddy and himself, just like before. And of course Buddy would attend. Hopefully this meeting was news that Jerry wanted to tell Buddy personally.

When Buddy walked into Jerry's office and saw Raymond Patriaca (the head of the New England Family, who answered to the Five Families in New York) himself sitting there, he was amazed. When he scanned the room, it was only the three of them, no muscle men, no guns, just the three of them. As they talked, Buddy telling Raymond about how things were running on the docks, Raymond was not happy. Buddy could see it in his eyes—the more Buddy talked, the angrier Raymond got. They talked for more than three hours, discussing territories and what to do about the McLaughlin and the Hughes brothers. This meeting was pivotal to the Winter Hill Gang's and Buddy's power; he had earned the respect of the best of the Italians. Raymond had been convinced that what he felt about Buddy was more than admiration—it was fear. This kid gave loyalty a different meaning that day. Raymond learned in conversation what respect and loyalty meant to Buddy. He also learned he was not a coldhearted man by any means; violence was always his last resort.

When they parted that day Raymond told Buddy, "I thought maybe I could persuade you to work with us, but now I feel we can work together." They stood up, and all shook hands. The meeting was over. Buddy walked out of Jerry's office that day feeling confident that things might actually change for the better now that he had the backing of the Five Families.

Unfortunately, he couldn't tell anyone of this meeting. If the McLaughlins ever found out he sat with Patriaca himself and discussed all Buddy's territories, even the ones Buddy didn't know he had, they would have been unable to be controlled, even by the Italians. The Italians liked Buddy's style. He wasn't like any of the brothers. He had something they didn't–compassion. Buddy helped anyone who asked, whether it be food, money, gas for the car, or just a pack of cigarettes. He was willing to give it just to save them from whatever might befall them. Buddy was strictly a family man. His family meant the world to him and always came first, so if the need was for family, Buddy was always the first one who came through.

Word spread about how Buddy had just walked into Jerry's office. He would walk by someone and hear things like, "What balls he has–just walked right in the office, no guns, no bodyguards, no nothing, and he walked out, was not carried, with no bruises or blood." The McLaughlins, after hearing the rumors, not believing them, were once again not happy with Buddy. Even though his strength was growing all by itself without the use of violence, everyone who met him liked him instantly and would end up admiring and respecting him. And once again Buddy became a legend. The McLaughlins were seen less and less on the docks after that meeting, which made Buddy feel that the Italians did listen to him. Also, Buddy did notice that a lot of the Italians were missing from the docks as well. Their presence was still there but not like before.

EIGHTEEN

Buddy had never considered being the head of anything. All his life he honestly tried to work hard for his family and give them a roof over their heads where they would feel safe. Buddy prided himself on doing a hard day's work—it made him feel accomplished. He always felt that he was one of the richest men not with money but with friends and family. He was proud of himself for how far he had come, a beautiful wife and four adoring children, a home any man would be proud of, until his close friend Joe McDonald was arrested. Up to this point Buddy didn't have as much as a parking ticket on his record. Actually, he didn't even have a record. He was well known not for his wrongdoings but for his compassionate heart. Of course, the police were familiar with the name Buddy McLean because of the fights he had had in Somerville. They were also familiar with the reasons and outcomes of these fights: mostly good clean fights, no police needed. Even if called they would not have gone. Buddy was known as a clean fighter and never really hurt anyone.

The police on several occasions did attend some of these fights and were reassured that Buddy was a clean fighter and an honorable man. The only thing Buddy would break on a man he fought was his pride; rarely were hospitals needed for his opponents. The police also respected him. They all liked him. When they heard on the radios that it was Buddy fighting, they really didn't hurry. They knew it would be a good fight and that nobody would get seriously hurt. They also knew Buddy always won. Buddy had, unbeknown to himself, some very loyal police offices, from patrolmen to captains, who not only liked him but had such respect for what he stood for that they from time to time closed their eyes to any of his minor wrongdoings.

Joe and his brother were arrested in 1960 for the Sunny Hurst robbery.

Although the gunmen were masked and made a clean getaway with $13,200 in cash and checks, four of the victims could pick out the robbers from photographs due to "red hair" and "crossed eyes." Leo McDonald of Somerville was identified, arrested, and held on $30,000 bail. On the day of his sentencing he received eighteen to twenty-five years for his part in the robbery. He openly admitted to committing the crime, and after he lost an appeal for a sentence reduction, his term was raised to twenty to thirty years. This happened because Leo refused to reveal the third accomplice in the robbery.

Joe McDonald was living in Malden at the time of his arrest. Malden sits adjacent to Medford, his home town. Joe received twelve to eighteen years with no change in sentence during all of his appeals. All this for a crime he didn't even commit. The second man in the crime was Allan "Suitcase" Fiddler of Charlestown, not Joe McDonald. Alan had been shot (but not killed) by Connie Hughes in front of the Alibi in 1953. The identity of the third man remains a mystery to this day. Joe was wrongly accused, and he knew the names of the other two gunmen that accompanied his older brother, but he never disclosed that information. Joe did the time and never broke the criminal's code of silence by ratting on the other two robbers. The code was very strong back then.

Buddy had worked alongside Joe Mac for years at the trucking combine in South Boston. Buddy and his five-man crew would unload the trucks coming into the fish pier. They were called lumpers. His reputation among the lumpers was excellent, a very hard worker and square shooter. It was always said his crew worked the hardest on the docks.

Both men were members of the Teamsters Local #25 in Charlestown. After the arrest of the McDonald brothers and hearing about the circumstances involved during the legal proceedings, Buddy threw a party, to raise legal funds, at the Alibi lounge in Charlestown for his fellow worker and longtime friend, Joe McDonald. The party was a huge success. They had live entertainment that ran all day and all night. It is estimated well over two thousand people attended the party during the course of the all-day event. All the proceeds went to legal fees and gave assistance to an innocent Joe McDonald, his lovely wife Florence, and their four children.

During the all-day affair, Joe approached the only man he felt he could really trust, the only man that had respect on the "Hill," the only man people would listen to. That man was none other than Buddy McLean, the Irish King of Winter Hill. Joe knew that Buddy was an honorable man. Joe also knew he was the only man who had the power to handle his affairs. He would ask him to take care of his small business interests in Somerville, and other areas, just in case he was found guilty. Joe's interests, as previously mentioned, were mainly rent collections (on various properties) and his booking operations. It was no secret that Joe had put a lot of people into legitimate business operations by lending them money. This money was alleged to be proceeds from prior bank robberies that he had masterminded.

Joe put mostly injured or elderly former Local #25 truck drivers in different businesses. Three of the businesses were small bars, one in Somerville, one in Malden, and one down on the Cape. Buddy agreed to help Joe manage his affairs if he was put in jail, which set Joe's mind at ease.

The two McDonald brothers were found guilty and sent to prison in February of that same year.

Buddy knew things were going to change for him drastically now. He could not believe the extent of not only his but Joe's interests. Buddy would now be head of the major bookies in Somerville, Medford, Malden, West Roxbury, Dorchester, and several other smaller cities, something he was not looking forward to. He knew collecting from these bookies sometimes got tricky, something Buddy wanted no part of. However, as the word of Buddy's involvement got out, the bookies started paying much better. No one wanted a visit from the King for payment. So not only did he control his own territories, but he now controlled Joe's as well.

The brothers were not too happy about this appointment; this would mean more power for Buddy. He already had the respect and loyalty of the longshoremen on the docks, and even the Italians in the North End liked him. And it seemed to the brothers that New York people loved him. Every time one of the McLaughlins would bring up Buddy's name, the New York guys would shrug it off, saying, "Ah, don't worry about him."

NINETEEN

The McLaughlins were getting very nervous, trying to take over as much as they could. This was infuriating for Buddy. He knew why they were able to take over as much as they had—they had to threaten and bully people into giving them what they wanted because all they had was fear as their weapon, not Buddy's style at all. Buddy knew he had to have another sit-down with Jerry. The McLaughlins were getting vicious and causing too much trouble for something they would never get. He would have to find a place where they could meet, a place where Jerry would feel comfortable. Buddy wasn't worried about himself at this point; he just knew something had to be done and soon, or he could end up dead.

He called his good friend, Mike Khory, the owner of Khory's States Bar on lower Broadway in east Somerville. Buddy told him he needed a big favor.

Mike said, "Of course, Buddy, I owe you anyway. What do you need? Anything, Buddy." Buddy said, "I need your place for an hour or so, Mike. I need you to unlock your back door on Tuesday morning at 10:00 a.m. sharp, and I don't want anyone in the place, just you till we get there."

"No problem, Buddy, anything else you need?"

"No, Mike," he said. "See you Tuesday."

Mike was curious as to who was coming with Buddy on Tuesday, and what could be going on. He knew better than to ask. If Buddy wanted to tell him, he would have.

Tuesday morning came, and Mike waited patiently at the locked back door. The knock came at 10:00 a.m. sharp, just as Buddy had said. Mike unlocked the door and opened it, and his jaw dropped. He stood there stunned at the site of Jerry Anguillo, no bodyguards, with Buddy standing behind him in broad daylight. He stepped back, ushered them in, then closed the door and locked it behind them.

Buddy turned to him and said, "Mike, we need to be alone for about half an hour. Can you take a walk?"

"Sure, Buddy, no problem, anything for you. I'll lock the door on my way out."

"Thanks, Mike," Buddy said, and out the door he went, locking it behind him. Mike knew if he looked in the corner window he could see what was going on without anybody knowing he was there, but he couldn't hear a thing. Oh, well, at least he would see whatever was going to happen.

The two men walked to one of the double tables, and as Buddy cleared the table, Jerry lit a cigar. When the table was cleared Buddy unrolled what looked like a map.

They talked continuously back and forth, smiling occasionally. Then that "I'm telling you" face of Buddy's came into his view. He knew Buddy was dead serious as to what was being said. He had seen that look before. Buddy was drawing circles on the map, first pointing to Jerry. Jerry looked at the map, pointed to something, and then nodded his head "yes." Then there was another circle, his thumb shoved toward Charlestown as if he were thumbing a ride. Jerry looked at this circle and decided it should be smaller. Buddy shook his head "no," and a few words were said, and Jerry gave the nod. Another circle, and he hit his chest. Now Jerry stood to look harder and seemed to want it larger. Buddy shook his head "no" again, and waved toward Charlestown. Buddy then put his hand on the lower half of the map and pointed his thumb up, as if to say, "Give it to them in New York." Jerry smiled at Buddy, pointing his cigar at him. I can just imagine what he was saying. Standing still mulling over the circles, each wanting some bigger and some smaller. Finally, it was done. Both men shook hands, and Mike knew some big deal had just been sealed—that was Buddy's signature, a handshake. Jerry agreed with this signature, knowing Buddy's reputation. He took his hand, and both men gave it a good shake. Mike couldn't wait to get back in, so he figured five minutes early wouldn't hurt.

He opened the door, and as he turned to lock it again he heard Buddy say, "I knew if we just sat here like two honorable men we could work this out without any violence and none of the bullshit, just two men talking. Now everybody will be happy with their territories and not one drop of blood shed."

Mike knew he had just witnessed something very important and significant, the Irish King and the Italian la Cosa Nostra himself, alone in his place, dividing territories. Mike was seeing just how powerful Buddy really was.

Before Buddy left he motioned to Mike, putting his index figure to his lips, saying, "This is hush hush, remember!" Mike knew what that meant—keep your mouth shut. Mike would. He liked Buddy, always did. When Buddy was in his bar Mike always knew there would never be any trouble.

When Buddy left the bar, satisfied with what had transpired, it brought back the memories of what Mary Hurley had told him years ago. Mary told Buddy that Preston, who was semi-retired, had properties in New Hampshire, the

Cape, and Florida, which were used as drop off sites. Many a body was buried on these properties. Preston maintained heavy contacts in New York, who were the main bank roll for the McLaughlin brothers. She also told him who many of the McLaughlins' partners were in different cities (the ones who were loyal to the McLaughlins and the ones who weren't). She suggested that Buddy should contact these men to join in and help him if he ever needed more help. Hopefully, with this meeting going as well as it did, things might calm down, and Buddy would never have to use Mary's advice. Hopefully, Jerry would take care of telling the brothers of their new territories, and they would accept his authority. But Buddy knew the brothers would not be happy when they saw what Buddy would control. His territory reached farther than the brothers could ever have hoped to extend to. Buddy had territories the brothers had hoped to gain, but the Five Families gave them to Buddy. Buddy also knew that this could possibly make things worse, as the brothers thought they had the unconditional support of the Five Families. Unfortunately, the families believed Buddy's story of what had happened in Salisbury, and they also thought the brothers were carrying this revenge too far. All the New York guys that had met Buddy admired him. He had respect everywhere he went. Any number of them would have been more than eager to have Buddy on their crew, but they all knew Buddy had his own.

TWENTY

It was in February of 1960 that a young Buddy, father of four and devoted husband, began dabbling in the illegal activities of his good friend, Joe MacDonald. It wasn't for the money or the power but to assist a friend in need. During that same time period, the McLaughlin brothers were busy with illegal activity of their own. They were still trying to take over some of Buddy's territories but were being met with plenty of resistance. They began to walk the docks again, hoping to intimidate the new drivers into paying a fee. They tried to bully and beat most of the new drivers into submission, with little success. Buddy or a member of the gang seemed to always be there to prevent the brothers from winning. As luck would have it, if Red Moran had anything to say about it, they wouldn't be doing it for long.

The appointment of Red Moran, who was known as an honest man who wouldn't go along with any funny business, put an end to any expectations of success that the McLaughlins or their New York associates may have had at that time. They were going to try a second attempt to take over the Boston waterfront, the first being in 1951 with the Pier 4 Brawl. Even the assassination attempts on Red Moran's life after he accepted the vice presidency didn't deter him from his goal.

The appointment of Red Moran was a blessing in disguise for Buddy. Now he would have help getting the McLaughlins off the docks.

Things began to escalate with the McLaughlin brothers. They needed to get rid of Buddy and as soon as possible. His following was growing, and the loyalty he had with them was getting too strong. The brothers started their search for an assassin. They knew it wasn't going to be easy for them, as Buddy was well liked and protected. Unfortunately for the McLaughlins, even some of their own crew members were loyal to Buddy. Had the brothers known this, they might have also been found dead.

After Buddy took over for Joe his life changed. Coming home to Jean and the kids was all he had to look forward to. Home was the only place he could be himself and feel safe. Just pulling in the driveway and smelling Jean's cooking made his heart soften. By the time he got to the door he had a big smile on his face—always. I remember running to him when he came in just to tell him what had happened that day; we all did. He would go into the living room and sit in his favorite chair, with one of us on his lap, and listen to us one by one. He always had time for us before dinner.

And the summer, I always loved the summer time—it was always exciting going places with my dad and having all the fun we had. I remember the fourth of July I asked my dad for some fireworks, which were illegal, and he told me, "No, absolutely not!" My mother, who was standing at the door, smiled. She was happy to hear his answer. Two days later, just as I was falling asleep, my dad came into my room. He crouched beside my bed and slid his hand under my pillow.

"Here, Michael," he said. "Whatever you do, don't let your mother know I gave these to you. She would kill me."

I smiled up at him and said, "No problem, Dad."

"Michael," he said with that look in his eyes. "Be careful." Then, out the door he went.

On occasional Saturdays in the summer we used to go to Revere Beach and ride all the amusements. They were always free, to us anyway. Every ride we stopped at, whoever was working the ride would greet my dad, always with a big "Hi, Buddy," and a handshake. They would then let us go on whatever ride they happened to be servicing. This happened even at the food stops there. We would get to have whatever we wanted to eat. I think my dad knew everybody who worked there. I can't remember ever seeing my dad pay for anything while we were there, and we always had a ball, went on every ride, played every game, and ate till our stomachs hurt. It was great. We would just be walking through the park, and men would stop him just to shake his hand. He would never stop to talk to these men long. I always remember hearing him say, "Hey, I'm with my kids right now. I'll talk to you tomorrow!" Everybody at the park seemed to know him and showed respect for him.

TWENTY-ONE

It was Labor Day weekend 1961, everyone was having cookouts, and the gangs were enjoying the long holiday weekend. Some of them stayed local for the big bash in Winthrop, and others went to Salisbury Beach, the jumping place to go that weekend, as Hampton was dry back then. They all hung around the local watering hole, the Royal. It was owned by a husband and wife, Joe and his wife, Butch. Both gangs congregated there for the most part peaceably all that summer. However, this weekend Ed, half owner of the Capitol Café, and Frank, a small time bookie, and his wife Alice, all from Somerville, were sitting at the bar when in walked Georgie McLaughlin half in the bag already. He walked right up to the bar and stood beside Alice and ordered a drink. Joe, the owner, saw Georgie and told his wife, Butch, to get some of the other patrons to the rear of the bar, cause he knew Georgie would bother anyone in his view. Georgie got his drink and offered Alice some with a shoulder bump, which almost knocked Alice off the stool.

Frank immediately said, "Hey, Georgie, be careful," but Georgie, just like his brothers, thought he could do whatever he wanted.

He leaned over Alice again and said, "You don't mind, do you, honey?" Alice, being nervous, shook her head no.

Georgie ordered another drink and leaned over Alice again, this time trying to grab her left breast.

Alice immediately slapped him, and Frank started yelling at Georgie, "What the fuck you doing, Georgie? That's my wife!"

Georgie, just being his belligerent self, said, "Hey, she liked it." Ed had all he could do to keep Frank from smashing him in the face with a bottle. But Georgie continued to harass Alice and started to grab her again. Alice leaned back, so he didn't get a good grip.

Frank started yelling at him again and Georgie sucker punched Frank, telling him, "Shut the fuck up. Do you know who I am?"

Frank shook his head to clear it, grabbed the bottle of beer sitting on the bar and smashed it over Georgie's head, yelling, "Keep your fucking hands off my wife!" Georgie stumbled backward and fell to the floor. Ed was on him immediately. Now Frank jumped on top of Georgie, both men pounding on him. Joe was getting nervous that they would kill Georgie. He finally broke it up and told the Somerville crew to go, that he would take care of Georgie.

There was Georgie, both eyes closed—he couldn't walk. Joe asked a local patron who had been there, a very good friend of his, to take him to the hospital and drop him off. They put the bloody Georgie McLaughlin in the back seat of his friend's car and drove him to the hospital in Newburyport, where they left him on the front lawn.

Well, the next morning the other two brothers got a call from the hospital telling them that they better come up there, that Georgie may not make it. They were told that Georgie had a severe skull fracture and swelling of the brain and that he was in intensive care. He had been beaten badly and left for dead. Bernie and Punchy drove up to Newburyport to see him and were told that they would have to come back, that he was that critical, and that they couldn't see him. The two then tried to figure out what might have happened.

Punchy told Bernie, "I thought he was going to Hampton to a party at some kid from Medford's house and that he would be staying there as well?" Bernie became concerned, knowing this kid hung with the Winter Hill Gang too. They drove immediately to Salisbury Beach to find the kid and get some answers. When they arrived at the Royal, they saw Happy Johnson from the Hill.

They walked right up to him and asked, "Where the fuck is Buddy McLean? And that kid from Medford?"

Happy, scared to answer, said, "I haven't seen Buddy all weekend. I thought he was going to Doc Reilly's in Winthrop for his big Labor Day party." The brothers were not happy. They wanted answers, and they wanted revenge. They wanted the blood of whoever beat their brother. Later they heard it was two guys from the Winter Hill gang who had put Georgie in intensive care. They were determined to find these two guys and give them the beating they had given Georgie, or worse, to kill them.

Buddy McLean got the word—the McLaughlins wanted a sit-down. Buddy was not happy about the situation, but his friends needed him to step in and calm this situation down, so Buddy agreed to meet with the brothers. Buddy chose the place, a place where he felt safe. He didn't really care if the brothers felt safe or not. The McLaughlins weren't thinking about safety at this time. They had only one thing on their minds—revenge.

When the brothers arrived, Bernie walked in first, yelling already, "What the fuck happened to my brother, Buddy?"

Buddy, knowing the whole story, tried to reason with Bernie, saying, "He was out of line, Bernie. He got fresh with a guy's wife while the guy was sitting right there beside her. He was way out of line." Bernie didn't care, just like his brother before him.

"Who were they?" Bernie continued to scream, saying he wanted to break their fucking legs.

So Buddy replied, "If that's all you want, I'll break their legs for you." When the McLaughlins refused his offer, Buddy knew then they wanted blood. Buddy refused to turn his two friends over to them. Bernie was bullshit.

He said, "Well, if you're not gonna turn them over to us, what the fuck are you gonna do about it?"

Buddy answered, "I told you before, if it will keep the peace I'll break their legs. This way you get your revenge." The McLaughlins were not happy with this arrangement and felt they were getting nowhere fast with Buddy McLean. This was the first of two meetings that the two sides had over this incident. In both meetings, Buddy tried to reason with the two brothers. He told them, "Georgie was out of line. Let it go. The guy was just defending his wife." But Buddy could see it in their eyes; the McLaughlin brothers wanted more. They wanted blood.

After the second meeting the brothers continued their search for the two responsible for putting Georgie in intensive care. However, no matter where they searched or how far they reached out for help, the two men were never seen again. The McLaughlins never stopped looking for them. Even though Georgie survived the beating this would never be forgotten, and Georgie would never be the same again.

TWENTY-TWO

My dad hung around the Capitol Café on Broadway in Somerville, and I used to get to go with him from time to time to shine shoes for the men who would be going in there. These men were always dressed to the nines, everyone more important than the next. I always made good tips from these men. Some of them knew I was Buddy's kid and would tip me even better for it. My dad seemed to know everyone who lived in Somerville and everyone who entered the Café.

At a certain time my dad would come out and tell me, "It's time to go home, Michael," and home I would go. I loved shining shoes there and seeing all the people paying tribute to my father.

When Buddy wouldn't or couldn't produce the two men the brothers got serious about getting rid of Buddy. They knew it wasn't going to be easy. Strangely enough, everywhere Buddy went there was always someone who wanted to fight him. It never ended for Buddy. Some of these fights would happen, short and sweet, but Buddy was getting tired of having to prove himself. As his loyalty strengthened, the fights became less and less frequent, which made Buddy very happy, knowing that he could go places without having to fight just to have a good time, and his gang members were seeing to it that he could.

However, these days everyone knew that the McLaughlins were out to get Buddy. And of course Buddy traveled with only his closest friends during this time, but unfortunately men began to disappear from both sides, everyone looking for answers. The McLaughlins were looking for a hitman, and the two guys, while the Winter Hill Gang was only looking to find out who the hitman was, so they could strike him before he could get to Buddy. They didn't care about the two guys.

Sitting in the Porter Sq. Diner one day, Buddy and his close friend Russ Nicolson were meeting a few others for lunch, a place they liked to eat. The old man who owned the place was receiving an order down in the basement when in came a group of young punks.

They started to harass the other customers sitting there, when Russ said, "Hey, leave the customers alone."

The punk started to laugh and said, (not knowing whom he was talking to) "Ya, what you gonna do about it, old man?" and pushed Russ. He laughed and said, "Gonna get your old foggy friends here to help you?" At this point Russ and Buddy got up to stop the punks, who were now egging them on. The rest of Buddy's friends got up to help when the punks began destroying the place. The owner appeared at the back door, seeing the punks running out the front door, and no one left but Buddy and his friends. They were trying to put the place right, but were charged with assault and battery and destruction of property. The owner was sure it had been them who destroyed the place. It seemed whenever they all came in some kind of trouble took place. Little did he know this time that Buddy and the guys were just trying to save his place from complete ruin. Buddy was arrested and charged. He immediately made bail and was told he would beat this, not to worry—they had reliable witnesses to the event. Buddy was arraigned, and a court date was set for October 30. This would be his first arrest.

A few days later Buddy stopped to see a few friends at the White Tower on the corner of McGrath Highway and Broadway across from Foss Park. He was sitting there just having coffee when a young kid started bugging him, saying things like, "Here we have a big tough guy, hey, people, here's the toughest guy in Somerville, the Irish King of Winter Hill. C'mon, tough guy, show us how tough you really are." He kept this up for several minutes, poking Buddy on his left shoulder. Buddy turned and slapped the kid's hands away from him, telling him to just sit down and mind his own business so no one got hurt. But of course the kid only got more vociferous, pushing and poking at Buddy to get up and fight him. Against his better judgment Buddy got up and hit the kid with a solid left, which sent him spinning. He recovered quickly and grabbed a fork from the counter and came rushing at Buddy again. Buddy laughed and grabbed onto the fork, trying to get it out of the kids hand. They both fell to the floor, and in the struggle the kid got stabbed with the fork. Buddy had no intentions of hurting this kid, except for the beating he was going to give him. This was an accident, but of course the police didn't see it that way, especially the way things were going. Buddy was arrested and charged with attempted murder. He made bail immediately and was released, scheduled to report back in court in late November. Unfortunately for Buddy, this kid of course came from Charlestown.

TWENTY-THREE

Attempts were being made on Buddy's life left and right. It seemed the McLaughlins were having a hell of a time finding someone who could do the job right. They hired a man by the name of Ronald Dermody to do the job. He was an ex-con just out of prison and ready for work. He was given all the details they knew about Buddy and was going to get paid $5,000 for the hit. The information included things like where he lived; where he liked to drink; what he liked to drink, in case of a poisoning; what his schedule was; and where he would most likely be at any certain time. The McLaughlins were sure that once they took Buddy out the war would be over, and they would control everything. They would have their two guys and would be able to take over the Winter Hill Gang.

Ronnie went to look at the neighborhood where Buddy lived, plotting his attack, when he saw him. Buddy was walking to the Capitol Café, coming from the direction of his house, so he followed him.

Ronnie reached the Capitol just behind Buddy. When he entered the Café he saw the blond haired man he had followed sitting in a booth alone, drinking his favorite drink. Even though he had never met Buddy McLean, he was sure it was him. The build, his coloring, and the drink confirmed to Ronnie this was his target. The man got up after two drinks and said "Good-bye" to the bartender, who replied with a "Take it easy, Buddy." He started his walk back the way he had come. Ronnie followed him, and once they were outside on the street he took out his gun and took aim on the unsuspecting Buddy McLean. Shooting him twice, Ronnie got him in the leg and in the shoulder. The man fell to the ground, and Ronnie took his leave before anyone could identify him. Hearing the gun shots, then police cars, from the back room, out came running Buddy and several of his friends.

Standing there, watching the proceedings going on in front of them, one of Buddy's friends said "Hey, Buddy, he looks like you." Buddy knew the man. He lived across the street from the terrace where he lived—Charlie, a nice guy. Charlie, however, did survive the shooting, and stayed off the kill list.

Ronnie, who couldn't wait to tell people that HE had just taken out Buddy McLean, called a good friend to tell him, but the guy he called was a closer friend of Buddy's.

He told Ronnie, "You didn't take him out. You hit the wrong guy." The very next day Ronald Dermody was found slumped over the steering wheel of his car, which was parked with the lights still on, in Watertown, Massachusetts. He had been shot several times at close range. It was assumed that the shooter was sitting in the passenger seat. Speculation was that the McLaughlins were not happy with the job that he had done. So many had tried to take Buddy out, but the Winter Hill Gang was too smart for them. The McLaughlins were getting desperate. They tried to get one of their men, who was also a friend of Buddy's, to invite him to his house for Thanksgiving.

Bernie was heard saying, "Buddy was never going to enjoy his turkey this year!" He wanted this man to poison him during dinner.

Of course, he flatly refused, saying, "I want no part of it." The McLaughlins were not happy but accepted his refusal. He was neutral and wanted to stay that way. They would have to try another way.

TWENTY-FOUR

Soon after, I woke up one morning to my dad yelling, "Jean, take the kids and stay in the back room." He grabbed my bat that was in the hall, and down the stairs he went and out the front door. Soon I hear the police cars, so I tiptoed down the back stairs and out the back door to where I could see police were all around the house and car. My mother was in the kitchen now telling the police that she had come down the stairs early to put on the coffee and noticed that the hood of her car that was parked in the driveway was up. This was unusual. She immediately ran upstairs to tell Buddy, who was still sleeping. Buddy told her to get the kids and stay in the back room on the second floor of the house.

When he arrived on the porch all he saw was someone running down the terrace and turning left, and then he was gone. It looked like someone he knew. He recognized the jacket but kept it to himself at the time. When I looked around the corner of the house I saw my dad in his cut off T-shirt yelling at the police, who had arrived in droves. He was standing by the driver's door. They were looking the car over. When my dad knelt down and looked under the car, he saw something taped together and wired under the driver's seat. He grabbed it out. When he got up I saw what he had in his hand—it was six sticks of dynamite taped together, with wires hanging from it. He began yelling again at the police.

When he turned back he saw me watching, trying not to be seen. He gave me that look, and upstairs I ran. He never said anything to me or anyone else about it after that day. He knew. I knew just by the look in his eyes not to say a word. I also knew we would never talk about this.

My grandmother arrived just then. Dad told her to wait there in the hallway. He ran upstairs and got his gun, came down, jabbed the gun in her purse, and told her to go home but without telling anyone what she had. She held her purse tight, walked down the stairs, and then just walked away. With all the police that had arrived she left almost unnoticed.

A police officer asked Buddy, "Who is she?" pointing to my grandmother.

"My wife's mother. I sent her home. She just got here. I didn't want her here for all this, and I didn't want her to know about the dynamite."

As far as he knew, no one knew about the dynamite but the police and himself, except for Michael, but he was the least of his troubles. He knew Michael would never tell anyone.

Of course, the news spread about the bomb, and everyone speculated about it, but all along Buddy knew exactly who had done this. There was no question in his mind that Bernie McLaughlin was behind it.

Buddy had his Porter Square Diner court case that day, so he would have been using Jean's car, while his was being repaired by her brother, who took it two days before. Buddy was furious. He couldn't believe the brothers had done this to his wife's car. What if he had gotten a ride that day? They could have killed Jean and the kids. This was getting way out of hand. This shit had to be stopped. He decided to go see Bernie and put an end to this bullshit—too many men were losing their lives just for their revenge. He would also have to see the Italians once again. Hurting his family in an attempt to get to him or get their own way was just not acceptable. Besides, Buddy didn't even know where the two so-called friends of his who started this whole thing were. He was determined to find out what it would take to end this, and that meant talking with Bernie. If the McLaughlins wouldn't stop, maybe the Italians would step in and keep the brothers under control.

Buddy told two of his close friends who were also charged in the incident that he wanted to go see Bernie during the break they would get in court. He wanted to end all this bullshit. Buddy called a close friend in Charlestown who was neutral, asking him to set up a meeting in City Square at lunch time, during the break he would get in court. A place where there would be plenty of people, preventing Bernie from ambushing him. Buddy got a call back telling him Bernie would be there waiting for him right in front of the Morning Glory Café. Both of Buddy's friends agreed to go with him, just in case.

The break had come. The three men piled into the car, and they drove to City Square, where Bernie could usually be found every day at lunch time. The square was always busy at this time, with the locals and longshoremen having their lunch break at the same time and with some of the longshoremen looking to get paid.

They found a parking space on Wapping Street near the square one block from the police station.

Buddy got out, telling his friends, "I'll be right back." They wanted to go with him, but Buddy told them, "I need to do this alone. If he sees I'm not alone it might cause problems, and that's what I'm trying to avoid." As Buddy went to get out, the driver grabbed his arm and handed him his gun, for which he had a permit. "Just in case, Buddy" he said. "It might be a setup."

"No," Buddy said. "We're just going to talk. I won't need it."

"Please," he pleaded with him. "You're going to be alone there. Do it for me, or let me come with you." To prevent him from coming, Buddy took the gun, stuck it in his belt and zipped his jacket. Buddy got out and walked through the square looking for Bernie. The square was crowded, but Buddy spotted him standing beside one of the steel girders holding up the el in front of the Café. He was with one of his bodyguards. They were right where his friend said he would be. Buddy met his friend, and together they walked through the crowd to where Bernie was waiting.

Buddy walked right up to Bernie and started to talk, saying, "Bernie, this shit has to stop," but Bernie didn't want to hear what Buddy had to say. All he wanted was the two men.

He yelled back at Buddy, "Then give me the two guys." Buddy tried to explain.

"How can I give them to you if I can't even find them?" So they started to argue again about Georgie being out of hand. Buddy tried in vain to convince Bernie that Georgie got what he deserved. Then, they argued about the bomb, which Bernie promptly denied, but Buddy knew better—he knew that Bernie had been behind it, that he had been behind previous car bombings. It was his thing. The conversation began to heat up, so they moved behind the steel girder and continued to argue, and it escalated fast, with the finger pointing and the in-the-face talk. Finally, the friend who had set up the meeting decided to stop this before anyone got hurt.

He got between the two men when Bernie yelled at Buddy, "You're a fucking dead man." Buddy pushed his friend out of the way, pulled the gun he had in his belt, and just as a train was passing put five rounds into his head. Bernie fell to the ground and rolled into the gutter.

Buddy then walked around the steel girder, calm as can be, back to the car just as he had come, got in, and said, "Let's get back to court."

The two men just looked at each other, wondering what had happened. They thought they heard the gunshots, even with the train passing. They were keen to the sound, but they knew better than to ask—they just drove back to the courthouse. This all took place so fast. Hardly anyone in the crowded square knew what had happened because of the train muffling the gun shots and all the lunchtime activities going on.

On the drive back to the courthouse Buddy told his friends, "I didn't want it to go like that, but I guess I was dealing with the devil." He explained to his friends how Bernie had been so stubborn, wouldn't listen to anything Buddy had to say, just kept babbling about the two guys who had started it all. Bernie didn't care what Georgie had done; they just wanted their revenge.

Buddy was back in court by the time the news hit. The police couldn't at that time do anything about it, because nobody had identified anyone yet. The police were actively investigating the murder. Of course, while Buddy was back in court, being cleared of all charges in the Porter Sq. Diner incident, at the same time the police were looking for the gunman.

The police station was right there in the heart of the square, so response time was minimal. When they did arrive on the scene, Bernie was still alive, but before he could identify his killer he expired. The only reliable witness they thought they had was the loan shark enforcer for the brothers who set up the meeting. Unfortunately, he could not identify the shooter, because he didn't see him. The other two witnesses were a singer by the name of Lynda Lee, always thought to be a plant by the police, and a twelve-year-old girl. Lynda Lee first claimed she could identify Buddy McLean as the shooter; however, after her boyfriend, who was with her that day, testified, her testimony was discredited. He testified they had been in the Café having lunch when they heard the shots. When they left the Café the police had already arrived, so she couldn't have seen anyone, let alone Buddy McLean. They also said in the papers that they had a twelve-year-old girl who had seen Buddy there that day, but her parents would not let her testify. This was later proved to be just a scare tactic to get Buddy McLean for this murder.

Buddy and his two friends were arrested for the murder of Bernie McLaughlin. They were put in a lineup, but no one could identify any of them, so they were all released. One of his friends was charged with carrying a concealed weapon, which he had a license for, so those charges were eventually dropped. All three men were released, and the case went unsolved. Only speculation remained. The police thought it was Buddy but had no witnesses and no evidence to convict him. With a lack of evidence of any kind, they couldn't charge Buddy with anything.

But the war would most certainly continue.

TWENTY-FIVE

One night, shortly after the murder, my dad came home, went right into the living room and sat in his favorite chair. We were in the kitchen eating dinner. He was late that night. I could see him from the kitchen. He sat with his face in his hands, and it looked as if he were crying. My mom went in to see whether he was going to join us for dinner. She also thought Buddy was crying. She sat beside him on the edge of the chair, put her arms around him, gave him a hug, and assured him that he was safe here at home with her and the kids. He looked up at her smiled and said, "I'm just glad you're all here," as he held her hand in his. She smiled at him, kissed him sweetly on the top of his head, and said, "Come on, come in the kitchen and eat with us. You will feel better." They both came in and sat down and ate with us like nothing had happened. Dinner went as usual, with all the chatter about school and homework and all. I could see my dad's face soften with all the talk, and I saw a smile come to his lips.

A few weeks had passed and many men had disappeared or just run away, and the body count continued to grow, nearing forty at this point, with many more unaccounted for. Buddy knew that the remaining McLaughlins and their crew were still hunting him, only now with new enthusiasm.

Buddy had to appear in court again this time for the White Tower incident. He was hoping he was going to walk on this charge, too; however, the judge he had was not as forgiving. Buddy's lawyer tried to explain it was self-defense. The judge wasn't buying it. He was going to make an example of Buddy and put him in jail. His ulterior motive was to stop all this violence and hopefully put an end to the gang war.

But by this time the Winter Hill Gang had become the most feared Irish gang in American history, run by the Irish King, James "Buddy" McLean. Buddy had loyal members up and down the east and west coasts and any place in between. Many a man did unasked favors for the "King," favors that were unsolicited. If anyone denounced the King, they went missing, leaving Buddy unaware of what was happening. Buddy heard the stories and most of the time had no idea who these men were, doing supposedly his bidding. If Buddy mentioned to someone, just in conversation, that he didn't trust a certain person, the word got out, and unfortunately that man would be hurt or just disappear.

The FBI tried constantly in vain to follow all the key members of each gang. They were taken on long rides for nothing just because the person being followed knew it, so he would take them on nice, long rides to nowhere just to fuck with them.

TWENTY-SIX

Now with the FBI following both gangs and the McLaughlin brothers following Buddy's crew, it made for quite a chase. This continued for almost a year until the FBI finally gave up and agreed to follow only the key players. This didn't change anything; the FBI still couldn't follow anyone—they were always much too smart for them.

Buddy was sentenced to two years in prison to hopefully put an end to the war; however, the war was not affected. The body count continued to rise despite Buddy's incarceration. Before Buddy went off to prison, he had to make arrangements to be sure his wife and children would be protected. He had to have another meeting with Raymond Patriaca. The meeting was held in private, and no one knew about it, just Jerry and Buddy. Raymond was happy to help Buddy, as Buddy had helped Raymond in the past. Raymond was glad Buddy came to him and assured Buddy that his family would be safe. He would guarantee it. Buddy felt better after the meeting. This was one worry he didn't have to take to prison with him. Then, he had to sit Jean down and tell her whom to trust and whom not to. She listened to Buddy's warnings and set them to memory. He wanted to reassure her that things would be okay when he was gone, that she wouldn't have to worry about anything, that the boys would take care of her, and that they would see to it that no harm came to her or the kids. And if she had any trouble, a friend of his from the North End would be there to help. He gave her the numbers and told her not to use them unless it was an emergency. He told her that it wouldn't be long before he would be home again, that he wouldn't have to do the whole two years, that he should be home in twelve to thirteen months, and that things would go back to normal, whatever that was. Jean knew in her heart that Buddy was getting a raw deal, that he was being punished for having a reputation for being a tough street fighter. Jean knew firsthand how these fights would happen. Buddy would be minding his own business, and someone would, out of the blue, start harassing him. They usually didn't care where he was or whom he was with—they just wanted a piece of the King.

Jean remembers many a night having to leave a place by the back door to prevent another useless fight. Most of these guys were wannabes, and almost all were drunk, or well on the way, when they would get their balls up and try to take on the King. However, Buddy wouldn't fight all who approached him, and he didn't believe in fighting with a man who was drunk. He would tell them, "Come see me when you're sober, and we will have a go at it," but they never did approach him sober, not one of them.

The McLaughlins thought they could take over now that Buddy was in jail, but every effort they made was stopped by the loyal Winter Hill Gang members. The McLaughlins couldn't even touch Buddy in jail, even with as many men as they had in there. None wanted to tackle Buddy.

In jail he continued to run the everyday business on the Hill. No one approached him on anything—they knew better. His reputation had preceded him in more ways than one.

In jail Buddy was also a "King." He had his own section where he had his private chef and all the comforts of home, almost. While the other prisoners fought over food Buddy had anything he wanted to eat. Buddy felt as if he were on vacation from all the stress of the war and safe from harm. His only worry was his family. He waited patiently every week for Jean to visit. She would come and bring him steaks and all the fixings. Jean's visits made the time go by faster, for every visit meant he was closer to coming home to her and the kids.

He met some very influential people while he was there, not that he wanted to know them, but they could be helpful someday. He became very well liked. Everyone knew he had gotten the shaft and was stuck there because of a judge who thought he was going to end the war.

Buddy met Jimmy Sims, and they became close friends easily. They respected each other, and Jimmy admired how loyal Buddy was to his gang members. Jimmy was very happy to be Buddy's shadow. He liked the man and would defend him anytime. Buddy had heard of Jimmy before this, and now his opinion of him had changed. He "knew" the man now and liked him.

Buddy also met Joe Barbosa, a cold-blooded killer who took a liking to him. Buddy was pleased that he had his protection. Buddy knew even in prison the McLaughlins wouldn't stop trying to hit him; however, all their efforts were in vain with his new acquaintances.

During this time the Winter Hill Gang continued to function effortlessly without the King being there in person because of the loyalty he instilled in his members. They functioned like a well oiled machine and remained the FBI's most wanted gang.

Joe Barbosa tried on several occasions to join the gang, offering his services to Buddy, who continued to decline his offerings. Buddy wanted to keep Joe as an ally, but his brutality and way of handling situations were not to Buddy's liking. Buddy had heard about what happened to Joe's attorney, John Fitzgerald. (Fitzgerald was beaten to within an inch of his life for losing a case for Joe.) And it was obvious the Italians were not on Joe's side either. Joe told Buddy of his la Cosa Nostra connections, which he thought would impress Buddy. However, Buddy had his own connections to la Cosa Nostra and heard they had no use for Joe, that they were just playing him because he was a loose cannon. But this information Buddy kept to himself, for his own protection. Joe continued to befriend Buddy, protected him without Buddy knowing it, and enjoyed every minute of it.

When Buddy was released from prison, thirteen months later, he stayed in touch with Joe, but he was never allowed into the inner circle with Buddy. However, Jimmy Sims was welcomed with open arms. Jimmy became Buddy's loyal shadow.

The McLaughlins were happy that Buddy was out. Now they would have more opportunities to get to him. But they were not happy with his newly found allies in Jimmy Sims and Joe Barbosa. The McLaughlins continued to try to get Buddy. It was rumored that Georgie McLaughlin hid in the trunk of a car and tried to do a drive-by shooting of Buddy but of course failed. All the while Buddy's gang was growing, and so was the body count.

By the time Buddy left prison he had learned things he hoped he would never have to use. He had gained friends he didn't really want, but you know the saying—keep your friends close, and keep your enemies closer. From then on, that's what Buddy did.

At the same time, Georgie was being indicted for the murder of a bank teller at a party. It seemed that Georgie, being the terrible drunk that he was, started a fight with the host of the party. Of course with Georgie things got out of hand quickly, and he ended up beating the kid to death. He didn't go easy when they tried to arrest him either. He continued to yell, "Do you know who I am?"

TWENTY-SEVEN

Soon after Buddy was released from prison, he visited all the places he and Joe had interest in to make sure things were going smoothly, and they were. This process took Buddy almost three days to visit all the territories both he and Joe controlled, and in the end all seemed okay to Buddy.

He was pleased that his loyal gang members had things under control and that Joe would be happy as well. Buddy continued to run his and Joe's interests even though he was fighting for his life daily. He would make the necessary rounds to the places where he had to only show his face to get what was owed. Buddy, while making a usual stop in West Roxbury one day, was told that one of the McLaughlins was in there a few nights ago, asking who was in control there. The manager was irate while telling Buddy how this man caused such a ruckus that he had to give some dinners on the house so he wouldn't loses some good customers.

He told the guy it belonged to the Winter Hill Gang, and the guy said, "Not for long—maybe I might just take this place over. I like it here." It was Punchy McLaughlin, who now lived in West Roxbury. Punchy walked everywhere those days. Having only one hand made it difficult to drive. The McLaughlins' crew was trying any tactic they could to muscle their way into any place that was Winter Hill controlled, but to no avail. With Georgie in jail they now had only Punchy to deal with.

The call came in the afternoon from Jerry, asking Buddy to attend a very important meeting in the North End between himself and Raymond. It would only be the three of them, just like before. Jerry wanted to make sure Buddy felt safe coming to the North End alone for this meeting. He assured Buddy things were on the up and up, just a friendly meeting between friends. Buddy at this time was concerned about the complaints he had heard about Punchy McLaughlin visiting various establishments that were controlled by the Winter Hill Gang, trying to muscle his way into taking over each place. He would discuss this concern at the meeting.

When Buddy arrived alone, he was not afraid. He walked in just as if he owned the place, and they all shook hands like before and sat in the chairs, which were placed in a circle. The room was filled with cigar smoke and the smell of stale beer. Jerry motioned for Buddy to sit between himself and Raymond. Raymond spoke first, saying that things were getting bad and people were disappearing like flies. He wanted Buddy's help. Buddy explained that the McLaughlins wouldn't give up. They wanted their revenge for Bernie now, and they were not going to stop till they killed him. Between Jerry and Raymond they decided to help Buddy survive. They would tell the McLaughlins to lighten up, that maybe this war was getting out of hand, but Buddy refused, saying that they didn't have to do anything, that he would handle it himself. Buddy was sure that things would die down soon with more than half of the McLaughlin crew gone or missing by now. Raymond was not so sure, and neither was Jerry. They wanted to assure Buddy that they were there if he needed them to help. Raymond explained to

Buddy the favor he needed of him, and Buddy gladly agreed to help Raymond. They shook hands again, with Raymond holding Buddy's hand with both of his.

He told Buddy, "We are here for you, Buddy, a hundred percent. Remember that," as he patted him on the shoulder. Having completed their business they stood to leave, and all shook hands again with reassurance. Buddy left, unharmed again. When Buddy got home that day, sitting in his favorite chair, mulling over what had taken place in the meeting, he had a new perspective on the situation, knowing the Italians were with him.

Maybe this war wouldn't last much longer.

But the war didn't end. It continued with the body count rising daily.

TWENTY-EIGHT

The McLaughlins were getting suspicious of Harold Farmer, their New York la Cosa Nostra connection. He was not helping in a way that they thought he should, so they decided to take him out as well. They were getting the feeling that he was protecting Buddy. Harold had heard Buddy's side of the story and was with him in the war. He couldn't tell the brothers that; they would have killed him for sure. Unfortunately, the New York guys didn't want to take on the brothers either—they just wanted to stay in it enough to satisfy the boys, not really enough to help them. If they had their choice, it would have been to back Buddy, but they were in too deep with the brothers to drop them now. Buddy could not be persuaded to take advantage of the little guy, but the brothers were more than eager and rather enjoyed it. They enjoyed the fear that they saw in the eyes of these men. It made them feel important. Little did they know that it only made the men fear them, not like them, and they would never give the brothers any loyalty or respect. The New York guys needed this intimidation by the brothers to keep things under control in Boston. They would help only if it benefitted them, and secretly siding with Buddy did.

It was a week before Halloween, and Dad came home infuriated, crumpling the newspaper in his fist, then dropping it on the coffee table. The papers my dad had in his hand told the story of how Punchy McLaughlin had been waiting for the bus at a stop in West Roxbury, where he lived at the time. He was going to see his brother Georgie, who was being sentenced for the murder of the bank teller. Georgie was found guilty and sentenced to death. At the same time Georgie was being sentenced to death, Punchy was being gunned down. Buddy knew this was only going to make the war worse. The remaining McLaughlin crew would now be even more determined to get him, not only for Bernie but now for Punchy. At this point no one knew who had done the deed, but Buddy knew he would be blamed. The previous attempts on Punchy's life were also unsolved. The speculation was that he was caught stealing from someone and was beaten and ended up losing his hand.

Buddy's loyal followers came from all over the country in places he didn't even know he had friends.

I was told by a friend of his, "If your father knew all the people who claimed to know and like him, he would have been elected president had he run." The more popular he became, the harder it was for the McLaughlin crew to get to him. They would have to plan very carefully if they thought they would have even a slight chance of taking him out. At this time in the war, Buddy rarely went anywhere alone—he couldn't. You never knew when or where the McLaughlin crew's hired assassin would strike next. Everyone was on the alert. Buddy had a hard time trusting anyone because the McLaughlin crew was ruthless. They would have tried to get his own brother to take him out, if they knew he had one.

TWENTY-NINE

I still remember Halloween night as if it were yesterday. My dad took us out trick-or-treating up and down our street. It was great. We went from house to house with Dad waiting on the sidewalk as Jimmy and I went up and down the stairs to get our goodies, with Lea trailing behind us. He kidded with us, telling me I made a great pirate, and that Lea was a beautiful princess.

She would giggle and say, "Oh, daddy!" Poor Dad had to carry Lea most of the way, but she loved it, and he didn't seem to mind. When it got dark, it was time for us to go in and have Mom go through our loot to see what we could have and what had to be thrown away. Dad went upstairs and changed his clothes. He looked great all dressed up. He was going to the Capitol Café for a Halloween party (no costumes). He also had a meeting at closing to settle a hijacking. The hijackers were giving Buddy his due. I asked if I could come and shine shoes.

He rustled my hair and said, "No, not tonight, Michael, maybe next time."

"Okay," I said and ran in the kitchen to see what I had for loot, and out the door he went.

Falling asleep that night was hard, with all the candy and goodies I had to eat. Finally, sleep came to me, only to be woken up by the phone ringing in my mom's room. I looked at the clock—it was 2:00 a.m., and the next thing I heard was my mother screaming, "No! Buddy!" Jimmy and I ran to her room, and she was sitting on the bed, with the phone still in her hand, crying uncontrollably.

"Your dad's been shot. They shot him." I was stunned and started to cry. We all did—we hugged and consoled one another.

Early the next morning my dad's friends started to fill the house, all giving their own account of what had happened. I tried to get closer so I could hear the story of what had happened because no one was paying attention to who was in ear shot.

It seems that my dad had finished his business at the Café and was on his way home. He was with two of his friends. As he headed for the car, from out of the shadows of the old theater came Stevie Hughes, shotgun in hand, shooting wildly at all three. My dad was about to get in the car when Stevie ran to the driver's side and through the windshield began to fill Buddy with gunshots. The three didn't have a chance and never knew what hit them. My dad's two friends survived barely, but they were not the target, just casualties.

The gunman dropped the rifle and down the alley he ran. He jumped over the fence and into the waiting car and then drove down Sewell Street and out of sight. Buddy was lying face up on the sidewalk and looked pretty bad. He was barely breathing. An officer who had arrived on the scene got on his radio to report the incident. They said that when the call came into the police station ("Shooting at Capitol Café" "Buddy McLean's been hit"), almost all the police cars on duty that night arrived. Several ambulances arrived, they said, all of them concerned about the condition of Buddy McLean, who was the worst hit. Before my dad was even removed from the sidewalk, the photographers arrived, all trying to get the best shot of the King, glass shattered all over him. But no photographs ever appeared in the papers, just the ones of the car, thanks to the Somerville police.

I moved to another group in the kitchen who were also talking about it, saying, "Didn't anyone check before he left the Café?"

I heard someone say, "We checked all night long, didn't see anything out of the ordinary." I wandered from room to room, listening to the stories of how each had met my dad. Sitting on the stairs I overheard two older men talking.

One was saying, "I remember the first time I met Buddy. It was in east Boston at Tony G's. We were in the back room playing cards when in comes this kid. With conviction he demanded, 'Which one of you is Tony?' Some of the other guys knew who he was and were all shitting in their pants, especially Tony. It seems that Tony G's guys had just robbed a cargo ship down on the docks where Buddy's father, Bill, was chief clerk at the time and would be held responsible.

"Tony stood up and said, 'What do you want?' Buddy got right up close to him and said, 'Look in my eyes. I'm telling you right now, I'll give you one hour to return everything, and I mean everything.' After he left, he told us that that was Buddy McLean from Somerville. He also told us how surprised he was that Buddy found out who had robbed his father so quickly, which scared him even more. How did the King know? In any case Tony scrambled to get all the goods taken back to the docks within the hour. After that day I liked him. He scared me, too, but I liked him anyway."

What I heard from a neutral friend, years later, was that Stevie Hughes and his brother Connie had been seen several times that night driving by the Café heading towards

Charlestown. When they finally headed straight up and out of sight it was thought they had gone back to Charlestown. However, what they had really done was circle behind the Capitol Café on Sewell Street, where Stevie jumped out of the car and hopped the fence behind the theater. He then slithered close to the building through the ally on the opposite side of the theater to the front, where he slipped into the shadows of the old front doors. Hidden from view in the shadows Stevie waited, rifle by his side, unseen by anyone who might be looking.

While waiting for the phone to ring I started wandering again, listening to different stories, some of which made no sense to me. Finally I went back to the living room where my mom sat waiting. She was anxious to go see my dad. Time seemed to go by so slowly that day, waiting for that phone to ring, and every time it did we all froze. My stomach would turn, and my mom would go pale, all the blood draining from her face, a look of panic on it. It was just someone seeing if she had heard anything on Buddy's condition yet.

"No, but as soon as I do I will let you know," and then she would hang up. It must have been torture for her, because I know it was for me.

At 10:30 a.m. the phone rang. My mom picked it up.

"Yes, this is Mrs. McLean." I could tell by the way her face drained it was not good news.

With tears streaming down her face she called us together and told us, "Your dad's gone." He didn't make it through the surgery. We all hugged and cried together, each of us hurting in his or her own way.

All his friends that were there tried to console us, but at that time there was no consolation—the loss was just too much for us. I remember people trying to talk to us, but I don't think even my mom heard a word they said. The shock was just setting in.

Being young at the time—I was only eleven—it was hard accepting the fact that he would never be coming home again. The next few days were hectic. People came to pay their respects to my mom and us. Some of these people we didn't even know my Dad knew them. Most would come with food and their condolences for the family, all wanting to know what else they could do for us. But there was nothing that could be done to take the pain of losing him away.

Even when the chief of police came to the house my mom though it was for more information on the shooting or to tell us who had done this terrible thing. Instead he came to tell my mom that the Somerville police would like to show their respects to a great man. Every cop in Somerville who knew my dad liked him. They told her anything she needed they would try to help. Just let them know.

I wanted to know all the details of what had happened, but they thought I was too young to understand, and I was also told I could not attend my dad's funeral. This was something I never understood to this day. All I wanted was to say "good-bye" to my Dad, to tell him how much I would miss him and how much I loved him. It wasn't till years later I got to do just that, but that's also another story.

THIRTY

For many years after that I tried to understand the thinking that kept me from my dad's funeral. I didn't know if it was the crowds that would be there, or that my mother was so distraught that she wanted only Jimmy there and didn't want any of us to see her falling apart, again. Even though they thought I wasn't old enough to go, I always felt I was.

His funeral was held at the Kelleher Funeral Home on lower Broadway in East Somerville. They had a police detail that covered most of East Broadway. The traffic was horrendous. They couldn't keep up with the cars coming and going. It was the biggest funeral ever held in Somerville to date. The Kelleher Funeral Home reported that more than five thousand mourners had come to pay their respects.

The Somerville Journal featured a five-page spread of the whole affair, from the list of who's who, who attended, right down to the pall bearers. The list seemed to go on forever. There were heads of unions, mayors—even a former governor came. Even the Boston police commissioner, Edmund L. McNamara, came. He was later quoted as saying, "During my investigations of the gang war it showed that Buddy had some good points. He was known as a hardworking, well liked lumper," said the commissioner.

On the day of his actual funeral procession and burial, they had to close Temple Street and all adjoining streets to the church. They had a police detail at every corner. The church was filled to capacity, with a multitude of overflow to the street. Besides the family car, two flower cars, and the hearse, there were more than thirty-six followers to the cemetery. It was a procession that had never been seen in Somerville, or any other city, for that matter, before this day. Two police cars and four motorcycles escorted the procession, with two more police cars and four more motorcycles following it. The procession took more than two hours to reach the Malden Cemetery, where Buddy was to be laid to rest. His wish was to be buried with the only mother he had known, Mary Raposa.

When the news of Buddy's demise had reached the corners of the earth, the Irish in Ireland who had heard of his accomplishments paid tribute to him. A song was written by Derek Warfield, called, "The Ballad of Buddy McLean," to honor all he did for the Irish longshoreman.

KMC

CPSIA information can be obtained
at www.ICGtesting.com
Printed in the USA
BVHW062133020322
630440BV00001B/149